SECRETS *of* VITO

*Very Important Top Officer

THINK *and* SELL

like a CEO

by the author of
SELLING TO VITO,
the Very Important
Top Officer

ANTHONY
PARINELLO

EP
Entrepreneur
Press

Editorial Director: Jere L. Calmes
Cover Design: Beth Hansen-Winter
Composition and Production: Eliot House Productions

This publication is designed to provide accurate and authoritative information
in regard to the subject matter covered. It is sold with the understanding that the
publisher is not engaged in rendering legal, accounting, or other professional
services. If legal advice or other expert assistance is required, the services of a
competent professional person should be sought.
—From a Declaration of Principles jointly adopted by a
committee of the American Bar Association and
a committee of Publishers and Associations

Library of Congress Cataloging-in-Publication
Parinello, Anthony.
    Secrets of Vito (very important top officer): think and sell like a
CEO/Anthony Parinello.
      p.   cm.
    Includes index.
    ISBN 1-599180-33-2
      1. Selling. 2. Chief executive officers. 3. Business networks. I. Title.
    HF5438.25 .P362 2002
    658.85—dc21   2002068375

Printed in Canada

10 09 08 07 06 05 04 03 02   10 9 8 7 6 5 4 3 2 1

TABLE OF CONTENTS

ACKNOWLEDGMENTS

I am thanking the following individuals for the both of us; you the reader and me the author. Without their help, you and I would never have had the opportunity to meet. There are many different hands and minds that have "touched" the book you now hold: the alumni of my seminars and workshops, who always keep me stretching and searching for new and better ways to sell; my customers, who provide the revenue, testimonials, and referrals that keep my business growing; Catherine Jones, whose efforts and hard work kept my company running while I spent countless hours writing; the many CEOs who gave their time and insights for you and I to learn from; my family members and close friends, who listened to my ideas and encouraged me; Heather Steven for reading, critiquing, and giving me love and support; the wonderful and knowledgeable folks at Entrepreneur Media, whose marketing, management, and production capabilities are nothing short of world-class: Neil Perlman, Peter Shea, Jill Juedes, Jere Calmes, and Michael Drew. The folks at Eliot House Productions smoothed out the edges, and cover design credits go to Beth Hansen-Winter.

Finally, a special thanks to you!

None of this would be possible without you, my new friend. Without your unique needs, interests, and dreams, there might as well be no book at all!

I invite you to read, learn, and prosper.

—Anthony Parinello

INTRODUCTION

This entirely new program, *Secrets of VITO:™* Think and Sell Like a CEO,* has nothing to do with my Italian heritage or my youth in Hoboken, New Jersey. Actually, VITO is an acronym I came up with more than 20 years ago for *Very Important Top Officer.* That's *the* person with veto power, the CEO, president, or owner.

This book has everything to do with the more than 100 interviews I conducted recently with the highly successful, maverick CEOs who run some of the most competitive companies in America. These interviews provide important insights on how you and I can effectively think and sell just like a person at the top.

You are about to take advantage of a simple but extremely powerful selling program. It is not for the faint of heart, nor indeed for anyone who is uncertain about whether selling is the right career. If you commit to it, the suggestions in this book will take you and your career to the top. The *only* way to make these ideas work is to commit to them without fear or hesitation.

I coined the phrase VITO back in 1981 when I was selling computers for Hewlett-Packard. Since then, I have won many,

many sales awards and accolades and have trained more than a million salespeople because I figured out what it takes to win VITOs as friends, business allies, and customers.

If you visit the sales offices of the majority of the Fortune 100 companies in America today, you'll hear phrases like:

Have you met VITO yet?
What's VITO's most important initiatives?
What's VITO's take on the situation?

Much to my surprise and delight, many of America's top sales teams know me as "the VITO man"! One of the things I've taught people over the years is that the following words are inter-changeable:

VITO, CEO, President, Owner

Whenever you see any one of these four words, I strongly suggest that you think in terms of the person's "veto power"—the power to say "yes" and make it stick when everyone else is saying "no," and vice versa.

As you make your way through this book, you'll learn three important things about the people at the top of your target organization:

1. They all sell the same way they buy and buy the way they sell.
2. They all share similar traits, demand similar results, and like to talk about similar topics.
3. Selling to these VITOs is a predictable, perfectible process, one that, when followed, will yield the same positive result time and time again.

By putting the ideas in this book to work, you will learn how to land larger deals, shorten your sales cycle, and win greater add-on business from your existing customers. How do I know this? I've spent more than half my life learning the process you'll find explained in this book. I've spent 15 years testing it in the field with more than one million business professionals at companies like AT&T, Compaq, EDS, Fujitsu, GE, Hewlett-Packard, Lexmark, NCR, Oracle, Office Depot, Sprint, the United States Postal Service, Kinko's, Unisys, and many others. The evidence is in: It works.

You can get to the top—and stay there—once you learn how to *Think and Sell Like a CEO.*

To my teachers and guardian angels
My mother, Josephine Rose
&
My brother, Alfred Charles

PART 1

SEEING THE SIGNS

1

*"The beginning is the most important part
of the work."*

PLATO

GETTING TO KNOW
THE CEO WHO SELLS

A re times tough? Are your markets more competitive than
they were a few years back? Is your competition brutal? Is
it taking longer to sell now than ever before? If you answered
"Yes" to any of these questions, guess what? It's time to change
the way you sell. It's time to find something new to stand on...
or, better still, to learn to fly.

There are, as I see it, three and only three
options for building long-term loyal relationships with buyers in today's economy.

1. Get your CEO to pick up the phone and
   help you sell by calling the buying organization's CEO, president, or owner.

2. Start acting like a CEO when you make
   sales calls and go on appointments by

> Change your
> career by
> changing your
> approach to
> selling.

3

starting your selling cycle at the very top of the organization. Do just what a CEO who sells does.

3. Combine items (1) and (2) above.

This book will show you how to put these "big ideas" into practice.

YOU READ RIGHT

No, what you just read was not a misprint. I really am talking about getting the head of your organization to provide "air cover" for you by connecting with the top people at the target buying organization. If you can't make that happen, take on the demeanor and world view of a CEO and do the job yourself—or, better still, use both of these approaches at the same time.

If you are forecasting earning revenue from a prospect or customer, you *must* develop a relationship with the person at or near the top of that organization.

That's the way of selling that this new world economy demands. It's going to take a certain amount of faith. But it's going to keep you ahead of the pack when the market is robust— and protect you from economic downturns when the market isn't quite as robust as you'd like.

If you're interested in bulletproofing your sales career, read on.

"BUT I CAN'T JUST WALK INTO THE CEO's OFFICE AND ASK HER OR HIM TO MAKE SALES CALLS FOR ME"

When your CEO makes a sales call, who does he or she call?

Sure you can. And if your CEO is anything like the hundreds I've connected with over the years, you'll get a fair hearing, especially if the company you work for is facing serious competitive pressures. (Bear in mind that a huge percentage of CEOs are former salespeople; my estimate is that two-thirds have sold in some capacity at some point in their career.)

If you decide *not* to enlist the aid of your company's top officer (or if you try and are unsuccessful), all is not lost—assuming that you have a little faith.

As you read the ideas in this book, I challenge you to *pretend that you are the CEO of your organization* in all but title—and implement what you learn. Apply the strategies, tactics, and technologies that you learn about here. When all is said and done, you will have adopted critical, revenue-boosting strategies that CEOs of small, medium, and large corporations are using *right now* to boost revenue market share and shareholder value.

> Surprise—it's fun to sell to (and from) the top!

If you're feeling a little uneasy about all this, let me share a pleasant surprise with you, one I honestly wish I was still in the position to discover for the very first time:

Selling to and from the top is fun.

WHY LISTEN?

I get plenty of flack for telling sales and marketing professionals that they have to adopt the selling culture of the CEO who sells. (And by the way, I've shared that message with well over one-and-a-half million businesspeople, many of whom work at some of the world's most prominent companies.) People listen to me because I convince them that if they give the system an honest try, they will find that this way of selling protects their market share, their organization, and (most important of all) their careers.

Whenever I tell a group I'm training that they really do have to take action and call each and every CEO at existing accounts—*and* call each and every CEO at each and every target company—I can feel the tension rise in the room. I can see the backs straighten up, the grips tighten on the pens and pencils. And I know the next thing I'll hear is some kind of dismissal or excuse.

> One cardinal rule: no excuses. (CEOs don't have time for them.)

Salespeople say:
- "Are you kidding?"
- "How could I possibly go over my contact's head?"
- "If you're not a CEO, you can't call a CEO. It has to be title to title when you're making such sales calls."

Vice presidents, senior executives, and midlevel managers say:
- "You want *me* to make calls?"
- "We've got highly paid and highly trained salespeople in place to do that sort of thing."
- "I've got to concentrate on keeping the sales team heading in the right direction."

Then the CEO (the only person in the room without white knuckles) says something like this:
- "Tony, that's a great idea. That's exactly what people at all levels of the organization should be doing. In fact, I've been trying to get people to mount just such a campaign."

And the room goes silent. People realize they better start listening to what I have to say. They start taking notes.

Don't wait for the CEO of your company to tell you this is what needs to happen next. Protect your company and your career by taking notes right now.

THREE QUESTIONS

Here are three questions to ponder.

> Selling like a CEO protects you from the competition.

1. *Have you ever lost a sale to a new prospect you were sure you were going to win—and found out later that the competitor who got the business was better positioned with a higher-level decision-maker?*

Most people I train answer "Yes" to this instantly. When they learn the real reason they didn't get the business, they realize it had nothing to do with price, performance, or anything related to the competition's offering. They lost the deal because someone else beat them to the true "approver" of the sale.

> 2. *Have you ever lost a big existing customer—one that you thought was going to be yours for life?*

Again, the answer is almost always "Yes." One horrible morning, we get the call from our day-to-day contact at Bread-and-Butter Unlimited, and she tells us the bad news: "I've got the word from the top: I have to switch to Brand X." We hang up the phone, and for the next four hours we sob like a baby. Then we kick ourselves around the parking lot for about two hours while we try to figure out how to tell our boss that Bread-and-Butter Unlimited is history. But do we ever ask ourselves, How could I have gotten "to the top" to keep this from happening?

> 3. *Do you have all the add-on business that you've worked hard for and deserve from your best existing customers?*

Let me guess: You don't. Instead, you have settled for small add-on orders from a few of your constituents. You've been knocking on the same doors because your current contact has you convinced he or she drives all of the decisions that affect your financial future.

That's two "yes" answers and one "no" answer so far, correct?

Are the wheels turning? Are you starting to think there may just be a better way to build long-term relationships that protect your income?

Good. Keep reading.

REMEDIES

There are clear strategies that will remedy each of these situations. I'm talking about "success steps" that

> Get the add-on business you deserve.

> If the CEO in each of your existing accounts hasn't heard directly from you about the actual value of your business relationship, you are at risk of losing the business.

> **What is the risk of *not* taking action?**

will begin a chain reaction and protect your company, your income, and your future.

You'll learn all about those remedies in this book. You'll learn them from someone who has been selling at the highest levels for 28 years and who has connected with hundreds of CEOs to find out *how they sell effectively*.

You'll learn that size, reputation, title, image, market share, time in service, and academic credentials matter far less than you imagine.

When you reach the last pages of this book, you will be ready to calculate the risks, focus on the rewards, and get the results you deserve. You will revamp your selling process and be tactically, strategically, and technically positioned for having the competitive advantage in the new world economy.

Congratulations. You've begun to learn how to fly.

Secrets of VITO

THINK

> ➤ CEOs know that the best way to get something done is to call the person in charge.
> ➤ If your CEO were going to make a sales call, would he or she start by calling a purchasing agent or an office manager? No!
> ➤ If you were to ask your own CEO whether it was a good idea for *you* to initiate contact at the top, what do you think his or her answer would be? You guessed it: Yes!

SELL

In order for you to sell like a CEO, you should:

> ➤ read this book.
> ➤ complete all the end-of-chapter exercises.

➤ connect to the World Wide Web as shown throughout this book.

➤ contact the CEO of your organization, share the most important points you learn, ask for advice, and follow his or her lead. (All this assumes, of course, that you yourself are not already the CEO of your organization!)

TAKE ACTION

Answer the following three questions with total honesty:

1. Have you ever lost a sale to a new prospect that you were sure you were going to win—and found out later that the competitor who got the business was better positioned with a higher-level decision-maker?

   Write your answer here:

2. Have you ever lost a big existing customer—one that you thought was going to be yours for life?

   Write your answer here:

3. Do you have all the add-on business that you've worked hard for and deserve from your best existing customers?

   Write your answer here:

If you answered "yes" to either the first or the second question and/or "no" to the third, you're perfectly positioned to benefit from the ideas in this book.

Keep going!
Don't lose momentum.
Start reading Chapter 2 within
24 hours of finishing Chapter 1.

2

*"Experience is a good teacher, but she sends
in terrific bills."*

—MINNA ANTRIM

OPERATING PRINCIPLES OF CEOS WHO SELL

I've met hundreds of CEOs over the years, and I've learned that CEOs who sell effectively share ten fundamental operating principles. As you read through the list, see how many you can relate to, you already have, or you use in your day-to-day business activities. Also, note the ones that come as a total surprise to you.

TEN OPERATING PRINCIPLES
1: CEOs Who Sell Know their Ideal Prospects

During one of my telementoring calls, a terrified salesperson asked me: "What's the fastest way to qualify a prospect? My CEO is coming into the office tomorrow, and she's asked that each rep introduce her to one qualified prospect."

What is a qualified prospect? Someone who *shares several key traits with your very best customers.* Look at the best customers you have and determine what five traits they have in common. When you look for a new prospect, make sure your target fits these common best-customer traits. That's what CEOs who sell do.

"Don't waste my time."

—CEO mantra

Never forget: CEOs hate wasting time. Time in the sales process adds to the cost of sales and extends the critical time-to-revenue benchmark. The higher the cost of sales and the longer the time to revenue, the lower the profit margin. So don't waste time talking to prospects who have nothing, or very little, in common with your best customers.

I told that terrified rep to do a quick inventory of his customer base, find the most common shared demographic and operational traits, and select the prospect in his "funnel" that most resembled his best customer. He did. A meeting of all three took place; the CEO was happy; the prospect was flattered by the attention; and the sale was accelerated.

Cut to the chase! Identify your ideal customer's profile. Then spend as much time as you can with only those kinds of prospects who are a match.

2: CEOs Who Sell Use Similar Criteria to Buy and Sell

CEOs take the same energetic, visionary approach to buying that they do to selling. I am not talking about finding out how CEOs decide to buy personal stock portfolios or how likely they are to dive headfirst into some new venture capital opportunity. I am talking about learning how CEOs buy goods and services that support their own core business.

> Don't call a CEO if you don't know what and how his or her company sells.

Once you see a CEO make a buying decision, you'll understand how that person goes about the process of selling. The opposite is also true.

For instance: The CEO of a medium-size company that sells a commodity product (one that is constantly compromised on price) will almost always ask for a price concession when making a buying decision. On the other hand, the CEO who sells the highest-quality product in the marketplace will almost always set quality and quality assurance highest on his or her list of buying criteria.

Could this information come in handy if you're targeting a sales message for or negotiating with a CEO? You bet.

3: CEOs Avoid Buck-Passing and like Having the Final Say

Whether they're negotiating the terms and conditions of a major deal or giving the "rubber stamp" to procurements, CEOs like to be in the middle of everything. They often take control of the purchasing process from behind the scenes.

Understand, too, that CEOs are unlikely to let the vice president of the department or the director of procurement off the hook when it comes to performing their work. But let's be realistic: When the CEO takes on the role of "decision-maker"

> CEOs get involved in everything. That's their job.

and/or "approver" of a critical transaction, the whole dynamic changes. The command from the top could be as obvious as "I've got the ball on the Thompson account," or as subtle as "Let me know when you're done with your analysis of the Thompson account— I want to take a look at your recommendations." (In the latter case, the person at the top wants the underling to still feel empowered even though, in reality, nothing could be further from the truth.)

4: CEOs Who Sell Personally and Consistently Model the Ideal Sales Process

Talk about a morale-builder. Everyone needs role models. Who plays the role of a model salesperson better than the head of the company?

The CEO is the person who is most concerned about the things salespeople are concerned about: revenue, efficiencies, protecting the customer base, getting add-on business, beating the competition, making customers happy, promoting a positive image in the marketplace, and so on. The CEO is also the person who is most passionately and intimately connected to the vision and mission statement of the company. (Of course, there are exceptions to this rule, but usually the CEO is Cheerleader #1.)

> If you've got a mission-critical idea, CEOS will listen.

Given these facts, why *wouldn't* you pick up the telephone, call your CEO, and ask, "If you were the top salesperson of our organization, what would your daily priorities be?" Make sure you've got a full pad of paper and a pen at the ready.

5: CEOs Who Sell Establish Personal Visibility within the Marketplace and the Community as a Whole

Imparting a touch of personal accountability and a sense of mission enhances the organization's brand(s), image, and reputation. The personal touch also shortens the sales cycle and wrings the most "bang for the buck" out of marketing programs.

This is true of CEOs—and it should also be true of individual salespeople.

Let's face it: Visibility builds business. The fastest way for you to confirm this is to look at the titles of the individuals who sit on the boards of the most important nonprofit organizations in your city. Then look at the titles of the individuals who are sitting on the board of directors of the most successful for-profit organizations. Notice any overlap?

> No one plays the role of a model salesperson better than a CEO.

Good CEOs network by force of habit and tend to make far more friends than enemies. (CEOs whose companies are competitors will often network and socialize with each other, which tells you something about how highly this success trait is valued.)

> What do your customers know about your product or service that you don't?

6: CEOs Who Sell Personally Monitor Changes in their Marketplace

There's nothing like talking to customers directly about how they're using your product, service, or solution. Leaving this to the marketing department or a team of consultants can lead to missed opportunities and slower-than-necessary time to market and time to revenue for new products and services.

Many CEOs track the reactions they get from small "focus groups." These groups are polled quarterly for quality, research, and development and "pumped" for other information that is fed directly to the CEO and then given to the top people in charge of the appropriate departments.

If you want to think like a CEO who sells, consider forming a "mini focus group" from your own customer base.

7: CEOs Who Sell Constantly Build on Interpersonal Relationships to Secure One-on-One Loyalty from Customers

Have you ever noticed that top CEOs send personalized, handwritten thank-you notes to each and every one of their colleagues at client/customer organizations? They do. I've seen this habit replicated in virtually any industry you can name.

> A well-written, handwritten note is the most powerful piece of business communication.

Again: If it makes sense for CEOs, it makes sense for salespeople. In particular, don't underestimate the power of a handwritten note! Notes can build truly extraordinary customer relationships.

This kind of correspondence should not be limited to the once-a-year "thanks for the business" missives.

CEOs who sell at (and from) the top remember occasions like business anniversaries, birthdays, wedding anniversaries, and industry awards. They are constantly on the lookout for life land-marks and personal accomplishments, and they send personal-ized correspondence when they see the remotest evidence of these in their customer and contact base.

Perhaps it's time to dust off and update your customer files and begin to set the stage for a new customer "touch-point" pro-gram that keeps you and your very best customers loyal to each other. The fastest and least expensive way to do this is to send that handwritten note.

You might also want to consider sending the CEO of every customer a coffee mug with your logo inscribed proudly on its side. This will act as the "silent" sales rep on the occasions when you can't be in front of your customers. Don't forget to include the business cards (signed, of course) of all the key people in your organization—including your CEO.

8: CEOs Who Sell Look for a Balanced "Gain" Equation

Do you think human beings are complex? We really aren't. We all either desire gains or try to avoid pain. That's the basic formula.

The most successful CEOs focus on positive end results like increased revenue, improved customer loyalty, and larger add-on business and intelligently balance these "gains" against the perceived (and often totally imaginary) "pain" of failure or humiliation that may be associated with efforts to turn these goals into reality. Put simply, CEOs keep their eyes on the prize and acknowledge that high achievement in life requires an acceptance of reasonable risk. They look

> Risk is a way of life at the top; risk assessment is a language CEOs under-stand. Always present your value so that the reward is stated in levels of risk. Never understate the amount of risk just to make your offer more attractive.

for the opportunities with the best payoffs and the best percentages—then they take the necessary risks.

Salespeople should do the same.

9: CEOs Who Sell Make Intelligent Decisions Quickly and Independently

> A CEO who really "gets" your value proposition may want to buy faster than you can deliver.

CEOs of buying organizations want to take action and buy just as fast as CEOs of organizations that want to sell. When a buying CEO understands the value proposition and knows how that proposition can help him or her attain a key strategic initiative by a certain time, you can expect action! Put this fact to work for your career.

CEOs don't "perch their pens" when doing so means missing out on immediate results. In fact, if there is one thing you can count on about CEOs, it's that they get downright vicious about missing out on *anything* that could make it easier or faster for them to achieve (or overachieve) their goals.

Selling to CEOs is simply a matter of consistently getting to the buying CEO and articulating, in a compelling way, *exactly* how you plan to help them overachieve a key strategic initiative by a certain time. Once you make your case effectively, stand back. Your target CEO will swing into action.

10: CEOs Who Sell Stay Focused and like People Who Can Do the Same

CEOs know that experts have a greater value than people who try to be everything to everyone. Not surprisingly, CEOs tend to consider themselves experts in a certain field. What's more, they tend to be right about their own expertise.

A CEO's expertise is the result of one thing: the ability to sustain personal focus in a given area.

In fact, by my estimation, successful CEOs spend about 75 percent of their "developmental energy" in a specific field of expertise. Twenty percent is spent on development of new talents that relate to their core strengths. Like all of us, they must spend some small amount of time—and perhaps 5 percent of their attention—engaged in areas that are outside their core competency.

> CEOs know how to stay focused. You should, too.

Take my advice and follow the lead of CEOs who sell. When it comes to relating to them, stay away from that last 5 percent. Deal only with the areas *they* care about, the skills and capacities *they* want to expand. Learn how to be an agent of change within *their* area of expertise—as an expert who complements their world view—and you'll earn a spot in their day.

Secrets of VITO

THINK

Success leaves clues—and so do CEOs who sell. As you read the following operating principles, ask yourself, "Which of these ideas do I already use? Which should I make an effort to transform into 'second nature'?"

1. *CEOs who sell know their ideal prospects.* What is a qualified prospect? Someone who *shares several key traits with your very best customers.*

2. *CEOs who sell use similar criteria to buy and sell.* Once you see a CEO make a buying decision, you'll know a lot about how that person goes about the process of selling. The opposite is also true.

3. *CEOs avoid buck-passing and like having the final say.* When the CEO takes on the role of "decision-maker" and/or "approver" of a critical transaction, the whole selling/buying dynamic changes.

4. *CEOs who sell personally and consistently model the ideal sales process.* Call your own CEO and ask: "If you were the top salesperson of our organization, what would your daily priorities be?" Write down the answer you get.

---

5. *CEOs who sell establish personal visibility within the marketplace and the community as a whole.* Visibility builds business. I invite you to look at the titles of the individuals who sit on the boards of the most important nonprofit and for-profit organizations in your sales territory. Notice any overlap?

6. *CEOs who sell personally monitor changes in their marketplace.* Many CEOs track the reactions they get from small "focus groups." Who are the members of your core focus group?

7. *CEOs who sell constantly build on interpersonal relationships to secure one-on-one loyalty from customers.* Have you ever noticed that top CEOs send personalized, handwritten thank-you notes? They do, and so should you.

8. *CEOs who sell look for a balanced "gain" equation.* CEOs intelligently balance "gains" against perceived (and often totally imaginary) "pain" of failure or humiliation that may be associated with efforts to turn these goals into reality.

9. *CEOs who sell make intelligent decisions quickly and independently.* CEOs of buying organizations generally want to take action and buy just as fast as CEOs of organizations that want to sell.

10. *CEOs who sell stay focused and like people who can do the same.* CEOs understand that there is intellectual and emotional power in putting every bit of your attention on one task at a time.

SELL

Take all the insights contained in the ten operating principles and put them to work *right now* on the biggest opportunity that you're currently working on.

TAKE ACTION

Ask your own CEO or the CEO of your best prospect or customer to validate, reinforce, or add to the ten operating principles outlined in this chapter.

3

EQUAL BUSINESS STATURE WITH CEOs

CEOs who sell, *sell to other CEOs*. What's the first essential prerequisite for doing that? Changing your fundamental assumptions about your "right" to communicate with people at the top of any organization.

WANT TO SELL TO CEOs? CHANGE YOUR HEAD!

Early in my sales career, I had the good fortune of being scared out of my wits. I booked an appointment with a senior decision-maker—the dean of a local college. The company I was selling for had just announced a solution for increasing enrollments at such institutions. Who, I thought to myself, would be more interested in talking to me than the dean?

As it turned out, booking the appointment was the easy part. What was interesting was what happened *after* booking the

> If your organi-
> zation has a
> single satisfied
> customer, you
> have the right
> to call a CEO
> at a target
> company
> directly.

appointment and *before* it was scheduled to take place. I got the shakes. You see, I was about to enter a world that was entirely foreign to me. I hadn't taken the time to get a college degree.

My technical training and experience in the U.S. Navy had been enough to get me a job selling computers. I knew a lot about my product. I'd met with plenty of purchasing agents, engineers, and data processing folks, but setting foot in a dean's office was suddenly an unsettling responsibility. What if this highly educated person were to ask, What college did you attend? If I answered honestly, would he dismiss me from his office? After all, I was "uneducated" when held to the standards of a degree.

I tied myself in knots in the days before that meeting. The countdown to the appointment was brutal. The closer to the date and time I got, the more nervous I was. I actually broke out in a rash.

On the morning of the appointment, I mustered my courage and drove to the college. I was escorted into the dean's office; as I waited for him to arrive, I scanned the various diplomas on the wall. I began to break out in a cold sweat.

I was seriously contemplating walking out when the dean

> You can add
> value to any-
> one's day—and
> that definitely
> includes CEOs.

walked in. My knees were a little unsteady as I rose to shake his hand. Are you ready for my opening line? It sounded like this: "Hi, my name is Tony Parinello, and I don't have a college education. I've been such a nervous wreck that I almost canceled my appointment with you, and I was just getting ready to walk out the door!" (Honest—that's what I said.)

What happened next changed the course of my career and my life.

The dean smiled and said, "Tony, take a seat. I've been quite nervous about meeting with you, too. In fact, I also almost canceled our appointment. The truth is, I don't know anything about computer systems."

Eventually, I closed that sale. But that wasn't the biggest victory that came out of my visit with the dean. The biggest victory was what I learned about my own talents and abilities. I learned I had the ability—and the right—to walk into any office and add value. I had learned my first important lesson about a principle I would later train more than one million others to build into their selling process. It's called Equal Business Stature (EBS), and you don't need a college diploma to understand it.

> Healthy self-esteem is essential if you hope to establish and maintain EBS with a CEO.

Here's the big question, though. What would have happened if I'd assumed that I had no right to present myself to this high-and-mighty decision-maker? How much would I have missed out on in that sale? In my career? In my life?

WHAT IS EBS?

- Having EBS means being ready, willing, and able to play on the same level as the person sitting across the table from you. (The same principle, of course, applies to people you call directly, leave voice mails for, or send letters and e-mails to.)
- EBS means assuming you have the ability—and the right—to change another person's pattern by initiating a new, mutually beneficial business relationship.
- It means understanding that you are the functional equal to whomever you are talking to.
- It means you have—or can easily attain—an equal understanding of some of the problems any CEO might be facing.
- It means taking the initiative to articulate your problem-solving ideas in a way that the top man or woman in a company or organization can easily understand.

- It means assuming the right to *communicate* in precisely the way CEOs do, regardless of whether or not chief executive officer is your job title.

> If you have, or can attain, a meaningful understanding of one or more of the problems your target CEO faces, you are entitled to EBS.

I was lucky. I learned this lesson when I was young. Most salespeople never learn it at all, and that's a pity.

Don't wait a day longer to master this lesson. Understand the importance of attaining EBS in *all* your business relationships. Never again assume you "don't have the right" to approach the person at the top. That's not how CEOs operate, and if you want to sell like a CEO, it can't be how you operate, either.

I've been selling to top officers for decades now. Here's what I've learned: If salespeople can make a habit of meeting with top people and assuming EBS, they will *always* sell faster and at greater volume levels than their peers and the competition.

When we connect with the CEO on an equal level, we stand a better chance of turning the person who has the ultimate authority into an immediate ally, sponsor, and coach. How important is that? Think about it. The CEO has the ultimate veto power for all the important decisions that will be made on any given day, week, month, or year within the target company.

Your sales career will soar when you begin to sell like a CEO—by selling *to* the CEO.

WHAT CEOs NOTICE

Once you've met with, say, five CEOs, you'll start to notice what CEOs who sell notice. You'll begin to see trends and commonalities among your new peers. You'll notice that the results they look for tend to be similar. You'll notice that topics they like to talk about fall within a few narrowly defined topics.

> Assuming EBS wins allies.

After meeting CEOs and business leaders in companies you're already familiar with, you'll eventually build up the confidence to meet CEOs and business leaders you know little to nothing about.

Please bear this in mind: *Fear of going to the top is an embrace of conformity—it's the desire to let external factors (like titles and flow charts and hierarchies) do our thinking for us. CEOs and other top decision-makers and approvers **don't** live their lives, or run their businesses, according to the dictates of conformity.*

> If "title to title" were really the rule by which the business world operated, nobody would sell much of anything.

COMMUNICATING WITH CEOs: PERSONAL STYLES AND BUSINESS TRAITS

Maintaining EBS requires that you know two things about any given CEO—the CEO's *business style* and the CEO's *personal style*. One is likely to vary more than the other.

Business Style

An essential element for maintaining EBS with a CEO or other top decision-maker/approver is an understanding of the person's *business style*. By "business style," I mean the way the other person looks at the world of work—the fundamental assumptions he or she makes about life in the business world.

CEOs tend to hold the following seven assumptions. In order to sustain EBS with any given CEO, you must know—and play to—these assumptions.

Warning: Some—and maybe all—of the elements of a CEO's business style can seem downright intimidating. Sometimes a CEO's image is so strong that you can't make out what exactly it is that he or she is trying to say. Rest assured, however, that one or more of the following assumptions is in play in the world of the executive you're working with.

<table>
<tr><td>

Check your
ego at the
door whenever
you deal
with CEOs.

</td></tr>
</table>

1: Knowledge Is Power
When these people talk, others tend to listen. And with good reason. CEOs tend to be keen and well-informed. They may not have gained their knowledge not as the result of a formal education but rather from coming up through the rank and file.

Ask yourself: Can I support EBS by helping to expand my contact's flow of critical information?

2: Passion and Commitment Make the Difference
CEOs all seem to have intense emotion about what they do. Their passion is contagious.

Ask yourself: Does my enthusiasm for the topic under discussion complement the CEO's? If not, you will have a hard time supporting EBS.

3: What's Good for Me Is Good for the Company
CEOs self-identify strongly with their organization and tend to feel very good about both (or at least project the image of feeling very good about both). In 28 years of selling, I have yet to come across a successful CEO who had a (readily apparent) self-esteem problem or openly doubted their self-reliance.

To put it another way: CEOs have strong egos. This seems to be universal. Top executives are self-assured and walk, talk, and act with an air of ability and confidence.

Ask yourself: Does what I'm doing support this person's best view of him/herself and his/her company? If so, you will find maintaining EBS easy; if not, you will find it impossible.

4: You Can Do, Get, and Be Anything You Want—If You See a "Big Enough Picture"
CEOs don't focus on tasks or tactics. They focus on strategies or plans. They have the ability to step back and actually see

their future as it relates to their current plan. They will change the plan midstream if it's not serving their ultimate purpose(s).

> Think strategically— act tactically.

These people take 50,000-foot views of the world. From their point of view, there's no need to get "bogged down" in "details" that represent days, weeks, or months of work for someone else.

Ask yourself: Does what I'm doing focus on the "big picture," as identified by this CEO? If so, you will find that maintaining EBS comes easily.

5: Good Things Happen When You Get People to Buy into Your Message

I'm not suggesting that every successful CEO is a great public speaker (although many are). I am telling you that most of the successful CEOs I've met—and *all* the CEOs who sell that I've met—know the importance of communicating persuasively and effectively.

> Seeing the "big picture" means understanding all the benefits of what you're selling.

Ask yourself: Does what I'm doing help this CEO get the message out and communicate effectively within the organization? If so, expect instant EBS; if not, be prepared to be relegated to the lower lines of the to-do list and the individuals who work that list.

6: You Can Never Get Enough Good Ideas to Support Your Plan

Whether the ideas are theirs or someone else's, CEOs love to consider them, *provided* they can connect them directly to the plan or vision that gets them up early in the morning and keeps them going late at night.

Ask yourself: Do the ideas I'm presenting directly support this CEO's plan? If so, you will find it easy to maintain EBS; if not, you will drop off the CEO's radar screen.

7: Results Are What Count

> Limit your topics of discussion to subjects you know to be of interest to the CEO.

CEOs keep their focus on what's happening in their own markets *and* in the markets of their prospects and customers. Why? Because they know they must deliver both *tangible* and *intangible* results in each of those areas. They have to deliver things like increased revenues (tangible result) *and* an intelligent strategic plan that positions the company effectively for the future (intangible result). (More on tangible and intangible results later.)

Ask yourself: Does what I want to talk about help this CEO create tangible and intangible positive results for shareholders, customers, and prospects? If so, you can expect respect, attention, and even (gasp!) telephone or in-person time from a CEO; if not, you can expect an uphill battle when it comes to supporting EBS.

Personal Style

In the 1970s, Dr. David Merrill made two important discoveries about personal styles—discoveries that are, in my experience, invaluable when it comes to interacting with CEOs (and the people who report to them). It's nearly impossible to maintain EBS without taking his observations into account, so I'll summarize them for you briefly.

Here are the two core principles.

1. People tend to either hold their emotions inside or show their emotions openly and freely.
2. When engaged in conversation, people tend to use either a dominant, "telling" style, or a more reserved, question-driven, "asking" style.

These two essential continua led to four (now-famous) descriptions of personality tendencies. All four are worth learning as a prelude to establishing EBS with any given CEO.

Note: People tend to have a single dominant style, but they may also incorporate more than one of the following four traits.

The Analytical Style
This personality type loves to deal with facts, figures, and details.

> Understand the four basic personality types.

These individuals are deliberate in their actions; you're likely to find them enjoying solitary activities.

They prefer a process in place of interaction with another person or team player. Accuracy and timeliness are their hallmarks. They have a low tolerance for mistakes, misinformation, and malfunction. They can be critical, but they do not like their work criticized by someone they feel to be of lesser authority, capability, or competency.

TIPS ON INTERACTIONS WITH THE ANALYTIC DECISION-MAKER AND APPROVER. They do everything "by the book," and getting the right answer is critical. You must prove that you understand the rules and demonstrate that you are willing to play by them. Never cut corners. Always understate and overdeliver.

When you make a request of an Analytic, never suggest that any element of the job should or might be overlooked, never imply that a procedure can be safely ignored, and never imply that any checklist can be condensed. Never ask this individual to "look at the big picture" or "forget about the small stuff."

Always respect and follow terms and conditions. In other words, have the utmost integrity when dealing with the Analytic.

> Rare birds: Less than 5 percent of the CEOs interviewed for this book were Analytics.

WHERE YOU'RE LIKELY TO FIND THEM. Professionally speaking, Analytics tend to hold job titles like programmer, engineer, scientist, CPA/accountant, and project leader. One might be a head scientist who developed a formula in the laboratory and is now running one of the largest chemical companies in the world. In other words: *They may also be CEOs.*

Think for a moment about people in your personal and professional world who fall into this category. Who are some of the Analytics in your life?

The Expressive Style

> Of the CEOs interviewed for this book, 25 percent were Expressives.

The Expressive loves dealing with people and teams. They volunteer to be in the center of any enjoyable and challenging new activity—as long as doing so involves interaction with others.

The Expressive loves change and loves the excitement that working with others on new projects can bring. In a group, Expressives are happiest when they're the center of attraction.

TIPS ON INTERACTIONS WITH THE EXPRESSIVE DECISION-MAKER AND APPROVER. Expressives may be excellent motivators and barnstormers, but they are often not strong on detail or follow-through. They may lose interest quickly and are usually not comfortable tackling complex, long-term projects or assignments. Note that, in most cases, being organized is not one of the Expressive's strong points.

It's not a good idea to ask for a detailed analysis or facts from this person. Forget probing for the details. The Expressive just won't deliver, although you can usually count on them to "hook up" with another member of the team who can track down all the details!

WHERE YOU'RE LIKELY TO FIND THEM. Careers that suit the Expressive may include marketing, sales, public relations, and communications. *They may also be CEOs.*

Leisure time may find the Expressive organizing or volunteering for a local charity. These folks are not loners. Night school, associations, gyms—anyplace where people are gathered is where the Expressive is likely to be. Who in your circle of associates would you identify as an Expressive?

The Amiable Style

The typical Amiable is caring, considerate, concerned, and always available for a friend or colleague. These people are great listeners and nurturers.

As a general rule, Amiables don't like to be in the limelight. They may avoid trying to introduce an idea into the hectic give and take of a group meeting. Instead, they may wait until the meeting is over and then track down a colleague and say, "I didn't want to bother you or interrupt the meeting, but I'd like to make a suggestion, if I could...."

> Amiables made up 10 percent of the CEOs interviewed for this book.

Amiables are extremely dependable and supportive. They will be ready to listen to you talk about how you feel.

TIPS ON INTERACTIONS WITH THE AMIABLE DECISION-MAKER AND APPROVER. Avoid rushing through the agenda in a way that alienates these people emotionally. Amiables are big on connecting and feeling; for them, that's the real reason for any meeting.

If you want something from an Amiable, emphasize what contribution the Amiable can make; always ask in a way that supports and respects your relationship with the Amiable.

Don't ever ask an Amiable to "take sides" or "stand up and be counted." Amiables don't like high-pressure situations. The tricky thing is, they won't necessarily tell you that.

WHERE YOU'RE LIKELY TO FIND THEM. Loyalty and listening come with the territory for Amiables, and their careers tend to reflect that. Common positions for Amiables are in customer service and support, administrative areas, and human resources departments. They also make great counselors and schoolteachers. *They may also be CEOs.*

The Driver Style

Surprise, surprise: 60 percent of the CEOs interviewed for this book were Drivers!

You'll usually find the Driver at the helm of the ship. Drivers love to lead; they love being in the pressure cooker; they love calling the shots.

Stress is their middle name; action is their game. They like to make snap decisions and sort problems out later. They tend to be short on intimacy and interpersonal relationship building but are often born politicians and networkers. If any of the four groups are attracted to empire building, it's the Driver group.

TIPS ON INTERACTIONS WITH THE DRIVER DECISION-MAKER AND APPROVER. If you need anything from the Driver, be brief, direct, and to the point. Expect the person to size you up quickly, make a decision, and move on to other business. Whatever you do, don't challenge this person's authority—in public or in private—unless you're ready for a major conflict.

Don't ask questions that force the Driver to admit that he or she doesn't know something; the exchange will stop cold. Focus instead on what the person is trying to accomplish and make suggestions based on what you hear about that objective.

WHERE YOU'RE LIKELY TO FIND THEM. Although it's possible for members of any of the other four groups to work at the pinnacle of an organization, the Driver is definitely the most likely to hold this kind of job. These people thrive in leadership positions. They make great entrepreneurs, senior executives, team leaders, presidents, CEOs, vice presidents, and business owners.

Think for a moment of people in your personal and professional world who fall into this category. Who are some of the Drivers in your world?

Important: In attempting to build an EBS with a CEO or other top decision-maker or approver, you could do worse than to operate on the assumption that many or most of them will be Drivers. Once you've confirmed this assumption, build your inter-actions around what they're trying to do or accomplish rather than how they feel; what flaw they've discovered; or how, when, or why they're next going to rally the team. (Those other concerns are likely to be of interest to Amiables, Analytics, or Expressives, respectively. Don't discount them; these folks are likely to be important team members who report to the Driver CEO.)

WHAT'S YOUR STYLE?

I am sure these four styles sound familiar. Did one seem appro-priate to your own style? According to Dr. Merrill, we each have a primary style and a secondary style.

There is no wrong or right style; each style is simply what it is. What's important is knowing how to recognize each of the styles and learning how to interact effectively.

In any organization, family, or other group, harmonious out-comes will be most likely to arise when each member focuses on his or her "strong suit" and nobody challenges his or her right or ability to do so. Let's confirm what your own primary style is.

Get a piece of paper and reproduce the simple chart on the next page.

Here are the questions:

1. During a conversation, do you typically have more of an "asking" or a "telling" communication style? (Place an "X" on the ask/tell line that reflects your style. If you ask more than tell, your "X" should be closest to the word "ask.")
2. During a conversation, do you typically hold your emo-tions inside, or are you more comfortable with showing your emotions? (Place an "X" on the line where it accu-rately reflects your behavior. If you hold emotions inside more than openly show them, your "X" should be toward the bottom of that line.)

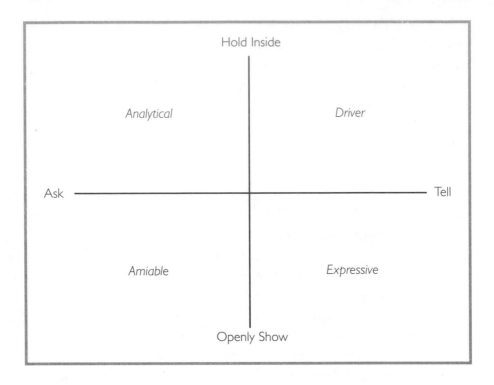

Which style do you tend to favor: Driver, Expressive, Analytic, or Amiable? Review your answer.

Now it gets interesting. Get a second and then a third opinion from others. This process of correctly identifying your own personality style is crucial if you plan to reach out to people at the top of your target organizations. It's important for you to get it right.

Have someone you know well on a social basis answer the two style questions with you in mind. Repeat this process with someone at work—someone you don't consider a close friend.

WHAT DOES ALL THIS MEAN?

Dr. Merrill put forth some interesting observations about this system of personality typing. For instance:

- "Like" styles do not necessarily get along or work well together.
- Styles that are situated on the chart directly "across" or "perpendicular" from each other generally have a more difficult time working together.
- Styles that are "up and down" from each other are more likely to interact harmoniously.

> Don't try to change your style to match the CEO (or anyone else). What's really important is identifying and understanding the other person's style.

Secrets of VITO

THINK

Having an equal business title means:

- ➤ comparing hierarchical placement and therefore power, influence, and authority.
- ➤ having similar responsibilities, roles, and reporting structures.
- ➤ enjoying similar benefits, salaries, and corporate perks.
- ➤ being somewhat competitive.

Having equal business stature means:

- ➤ having the right to communicate with anyone you choose, regardless of title.
- ➤ having the ability to articulate problem-solving ideas in such a way that anyone of any title can easily understand.
- ➤ developing mutually and equally beneficial business interactions and relationships.

You must maintain a business environment whereby EBS is established and maintained at all levels within your prospect's and customers' organizations.

SELL

You must be well-informed to sell to the CEO. You must:

> understand the industry you sell to.
> know how your products, services, and solutions solve problems that your target CEO cares about.
> be totally familiar with your target CEO's current vision and mission statement.

You must be passionate about your purpose.

> CEOs have an intense emotion about their company and the over-achievement of goals, plans, and objectives.
> Your passion must closely match that of the CEO's buying organization's.

TAKE ACTION

1. *Create a target CEO list.* Make a list containing the biggest opportunities that are currently in your sales forecast. Include the names of each CEO. As you read this book, quickly apply what you learn to each account and CEO.
2. *Choose a top-ten list.* Make a list of ten people you know well, and classify each person's dominant personal style. By doing so you'll be able to more easily identify the social styles of the CEOs you'll be selling to.
3. *Determine your social style.* Take the time to find out if you're a Driver, an Analytic, an Expressive, or an Amiable.
4. *Review all seven.* Take another look at the seven business style assumptions. Identify at least three ways you can support each one with your product, service, or solution for one of your target CEOs.

For additional information and worksheets, visit:
www.CEOsellingtips.com
Click on: "Get Info"
Locate and download Chapter 3.

4

"A study of economics usually reveals that the best time to buy anything is last year."

MARTY ALLEN

BEFORE CEOS BUY

We've seen that CEOs who sell target other CEOs and that selling to CEOs means having the courage and knowledge necessary to win, and keep, Equal Business Stature, or EBS. Now we have to examine the reasons the CEOs we're targeting actually *make buying decisions*—or allow them to be made, which is much the same thing.

There are three elements to consider: *knowledge, action,* and *currency.*

KNOWLEDGE

If a successful CEO is going to buy from you, he or she has to see that your plan reflects the right *knowledge.*

I am not talking about product knowledge here, although that is certainly important. Most CEOs don't spend their day focused on that kind of knowledge.

The kind of knowledge I'm talking about concerns the *strategic goals* that determine where a CEO's organization is heading in the market. This is information usually reflected in the strategic plan, which is an overview of the approach that will be used to get the company's products, services, and solutions out to customers. This document offers "big picture" answers to the question, What are we trying to do here?

Yes, it's true. In order for you to sell *your* stuff to the CEO, you have to be sure that what you offer matches the CEO's "big-picture" goals for selling *his* or *her* stuff!

CEOs must know, for example: What possible impact to the plan could result if focused, direct-mail campaigns are used? Will advertising support the mail campaign? Will telemarketing play a role in identifying potential customers? Will automatic voice-mail messaging be used in the business-to-consumer model? Will e-mail campaigns support all these efforts? Will the organization invest in trade shows and conventions? If so, who will attend? Will a partner or reseller channel be developed? Is one already in place? Who else will support the direct-sales force? How?

> Strategic goals and strategic thinking are analogous to the plans necessary to build a house. Imagine living in a home that was built without plans.

Most salespeople don't bother finding out this kind of information about their customers or prospects. If you're targeting a CEO, though, you must know the strategic plan of his or her organization. In order to sell like a CEO, you have to think like a CEO; you have to face up to the same challenges your target market faces and look at the tough questions in the same way they do.

> Be ready to ask: "What are the three most important elements of your strategic plan that you would like to see improved in the next 90 days?"

How do you learn about all this? For a start, take your own company's vice president of marketing out to lunch. Even better, spend some time in his or her world. Sit in on a few marketing brainstorm sessions (don't be surprised if you see your own CEO dropping in on one of these meetings unexpectedly; that's how they find out what's going on). Be a fly on the wall. Take lots of notes. Afterward, when the meeting has ended, ask some intelligent questions.

The strategic plan may be difficult or easy for you to track down from the outside. The point is, whatever value proposition you or your team ultimately makes to the CEO or other senior decision-maker/approver, it should be rooted in your *knowledge* of the target company's strategic plan. Whether you get that knowledge from news reports, independent phone research, or (my favorite) face-to-face meetings with CEOs, you will need to get it somehow.

ACTION

If CEOs are going to buy from you, they have to see that your plan supports their company's *actions* to implement their strategic plan.

> The tactical plan includes the actual steps that must be taken to accomplish the CEO's strategic goals.

What, specifically, is the target company going to do to turn its strategic goals into reality? If you have the answer to that question, you can build your approach around the action the CEO's company plans to take.

Again, if you want to sell like a CEO, you must have an understanding of the overall tactical plan, then find a way to support that plan.

The details of a target company's tactical plan are usually hard to get if you start your sales work at the middle or the bottom of the organization but ridiculously easy to get if you start at the top of the organization, with the CEO. This is one of the reasons sales cycles tend to be so much shorter for CEOs who sell (and salespeople who model their techniques). When a CEO meets with another CEO, it typically results in the buying organization's top person picking up the phone, calling the vice president of marketing, and saying something like, "I'm talking with Jane Smart, CEO of Brilliant Corporation. I want you to fill her people in on everything we're doing to penetrate the consumer market." If the top person takes your organization on as an ally, you get the information you need—*fast*.

If, on the other hand, you start out by calling the vice president of marketing and asking for a copy of the tactical plan, you may spend a month swapping voice-mail messages and even then may not get half the information you need.

To win the action part of the equation in a timely fashion, you have to be willing to start at the top—or, at the very least, to get your own CEO to help you start at the top.

> CEOs constantly raise their expectations with regard to the strategic plan; their tactical plans are usually in a state of flux.

CURRENCY

If a CEO is going to buy from you, he or she has to agree that your plan is part of a *current priority* for implementing the strategic plan.

This is the tricky one.

Each and every successful CEO has a set of priorities for daily action supporting the strategic plan. When someone proposes an idea that is a perfect match with a current priority of the CEO, that idea tends to get implemented quickly. When someone proposes an idea that falls into a gray area, or that actually *conflicts* with a CEO's current priority, ominous silence tends to ensue.

We've all seen it happen. Everything seems to be in place for a buy recommendation with a midlevel buyer and then—for no discernible reason—nothing happens. And nothing continues to happen for a very long time. This cycle often plays out simply because the midlevel decision-maker has made a suggestion that isn't a current priority for the buying organization's CEO—or is in direct conflict with something that is.

Secrets of VITO

THINK

If you're targeting a CEO, you must know the strategic and tactical plans of his or her organization.

Look for these important points about your target CEO's company:

> ➤ What has been the company's marketplace performance? Growth, level-line, or recession?

> ➤ Who are the company's biggest competitors? What's been their marketplace performance?

> ➤ Where have you heard about this company? (Trade publications, direct mail, TV ads, radio spots, billboards, newspapers?)

Look for these important points about your own company:

> ➤ Does your "big-picture" marketing strategy have any elements in common with the marketing strategies of your target CEO?

> ➤ Do your tactical take-to-market plans (for instance, advertising, sales channels) use any of the same methods of your target CEO?

The more matches you have, the easier it will be to establish a business relationship with your target CEO's organization.

SELL

Understand that if a CEO is going to buy from you, he or she has to agree that your product's results are a *current priority* that's critical to the overall success of key goals, plans, and objectives.

Look at:

➤ The target company's current level of loyalty to the current source of supply.

➤ Whether what you sell crosses departmental or divisional lines, affects revenue-generating abilities, has to do with effectiveness, or has the potential to cut nonvalue expense levels. If there's a "yes" answer anywhere in here, you can expect the CEO to get involved in the sale, visibly or otherwise.

➤ The current take-to-market and time-to-revenue periods. Long, drawn-out sales cycles don't appeal to buying or selling organizations.

TAKE ACTION

➤ Learn *your own company's* strategic plan backward and forward. (Your target CEOs won't have much respect for you if you don't.)

➤ Learn at least five key elements of *your own company's* tactical plan. (Ditto.)

➤ Review all three strategies for resolving "currency" problems with *your own company's* CEO; ask for his or her help as the need may arise. (You may be surprised at the enthusiasm of the positive response you receive.)

PART 2

BEHIND CLOSED
DOORS

5

---

*"Not everything that can be counted counts, and
not everything that counts can be counted."*

—ALBERT EINSTEIN

REACHING
OUT TO CEOS

T he new world economy in which all CEOs must operate
requires new tactical approaches for both selling and
procuring.

In this chapter, you'll learn how to use proven tactics combined with today's technology to package and deliver compelling
initial messages, value propositions, and presentations to people
at the top.

THE CONTACT SPORT OF CEO SELLING

I'm a far cry from being a sports enthusiast. As a matter of fact,
I'm sports-illiterate. I do know the meaning of the term "Monday
morning quarterback," though. It's used to describe people who'd
rather critique the actions of others after the fact than take action
themselves while those actions can still make a difference.

CEOs who sell don't fall into that category. They love being in the game, and they want to *stay* in the game. If you want to sell to them, you'll need to adopt their mind-set, take some chances, and do what you can to "move the ball forward" in each and every business relationship.

I will be giving you "plays" that work in opening up relationships in the ways that CEOs who sell open up relationships. No play works all the time, but some work a heck of a lot better over time than others do.

Use the ideas below. Stick with them. Don't fall into "shoulda, woulda, coulda" mode when the opposition shuts you down (which it will from time to time). Run the next play. If you do that consistently, your time-to-revenue figures will shrink, and you'll build new relationships with people at the very highest levels of the organization. You'll be selling the way CEOs sell.

HOW TO REACH OUT TO CEOs
(LIKE CEOs REACH OUT TO CEOs)

The strategy is simple: *Hit their hot buttons,* regardless of whether you reach out by letter, fax, e-mail, or voice mail.

> If you master the CEO's *hot buttons*, you will be perceived as speaking that CEO's language.

This is a secret that most salespeople overlook. The hot button is probably more important than the medium used to establish contact. Some people ask me, "Should I make cold calls or send e-mails?" The best answer is probably *both* (if you know how to push the CEO's hot button) and *neither* (if you don't).

Hot Button 1: The Balanced Reward Equation

Every CEO I interviewed related instantly to this guiding principle. If you hope to connect with CEOs, you *must* master the balanced reward equation—no ifs, ands, or buts.

The balanced reward equation offers a look at both the upside gain *and* the downside risk of any decision a CEO faces. It shows the whole picture and instantly earns top-of-mind awareness from any CEO who encounters it. (This is because most of the people who recommend things to CEOs *don't bother* to incorporate the downside of a decision, and CEOs get used to having to *ask* about that downside.)

> CEOs in similar industries have similar hot buttons.

People who run companies get used to hearing only one side of a story. People who run *successful* companies make a habit of finding out about both sides of a story.

In order to put together a balanced reward equation, we must understand some of the financial motivators that concern CEOs. There are four to consider.

Return on Assets (ROA)

Organizations have capital assets and human assets to account for. Capital assets tend to depreciate (get less valuable) over certain periods of time, and human assets tend to appreciate (get more valuable) over certain periods of time. What we need to add to this ROA equation is an organization's electronic assets. Electronic assets are considered to be the enterprisewide intranet (used to circulate and share information *internally*) and the electronic commerce of the organization's web site, which is used to communicate *externally*. Electronic assets may appreciate or depreciate, or may even appear to do both at the same time, depending on which you're measuring and in what context.

> CEOs appreciate honesty. Be realistic in your assumptions and projections.

Return on Sales (ROS)

This simply means the amount of net income expressed as a percentage of revenue. If sales increase and expenses that are related to sales stay the same, ROS goes up. If sales are flat and expenses that are related to sales go down, ROS goes up. If sales increase and expenses drop, the CEO looks like a genius.

CEOs can increase ROS by employing one or more of the following strategies:

- Increase prices.
- Increase the effectiveness and efficiency of the sales force.
- Reduce salaries and other expenses.

Return on Knowledge (ROK)

This is harder to measure at times but just as important as the other two.

About 80 percent of today's employees are knowledge-based workers; CEOs spend about 15 percent of their company's revenue in direct support of these knowledge-based workers. *Anything* that eats up 15 cents on the dollar is considered a big deal in the world of a CEO.

Net Working Capital (NWC)

It takes cash to run any organization. There are lots of ways to get this cash; some are more attractive to CEOs than others.

I'll assume for a minute that you're not a banker or a venture capitalist. Given that, the best way for you to help your prospect's organization generate cash is to find a way to compress its accounts receivables file. In other words, help your customers collect their money more quickly.

If your ideas can help reduce time-to-collection periods, and if those ideas can be sustained over a long period of time, you'll have a positive impact on net working capital, and that, in turn, will enhance the target company's value; if it's a publicly held company, you'll be enhancing shareholder value. Not surprisingly, that's what many CEOs dream about doing.

Two Types of Value

Before we can create an equation that a CEO will be immediately interested in learning more about, we must identify the two components that will be incorporated into the equation. These components must articulate value. Value comes in two forms: tangible and intangible.

Tangible value is easy to see and measure. A 5 percent increase in revenues, a 24 percent increase in personal productivity, a reduction in time-to-market by an average of 30 days, a lowering of expenses by 25 percent— these are all examples of tangible value. As you can see, tangible value is articulated using numbers.

> Be ready to ask: "What's changed in the past x months that is having a negative effect on the attainment of my goals?"

Can't deliver tangible value? Don't despair. CEOs get just as excited when they see a balanced reward equation that's built on *intangible* value—value that's harder to measure but still important in the CEO's daily routine. Examples include less risk of losing key employees to the competition, less worry about downtime during the busy season, a better image in the marketplace, improved labor relations, enhanced employee attitude toward the company, and so on.

Unlike tangible value, intangible value is articulated primarily by means of descriptive words and phrases. Numbers don't play a role.

Let's Balance an Equation

Now it's time to create and test a balanced reward equation.

Again, don't be concerned with *how* a target CEO will read, hear, or see this statement. It doesn't matter. Once you create the right equation, you can package it in just about any form. You'll be *speaking the language of CEOs*, and that's what will matter most.

Let's start out by looking at what we *don't* want to do. Here's a statement based on tangible value that is *not* balanced.

Overachieve your revenue goals by 15 percent!

This demands quite a lot—in fact, too much—from the imagination. The call to action leaves too many questions unanswered for a self-respecting CEO to take seriously. What, exactly, has to be done to get this result? Must marketing budgets be increased to perform additional advertising? Do we need to revamp our sales compensation plan and offer higher bonuses for certain products? Must we bring on more administrative staff to support presales activities? All these concerns cast a cloud of suspicion over the benefit claim.

Consider this: A good CEO probably *already knows* how to overachieve revenue goals by (at least) 15 percent. Piece of cake! Just hire a fancy advertising agency and launch a national advertising campaign (to use one possible example). *But:* Would the company be able to do so profitably? That, of course, is another question entirely. It's in having to resolve *both* types of questions, usually at the same time, that CEOs distinguish themselves from the rest of the business world. *If you want to sell like CEOs, you must think like CEOs do and only pose benefits that "look both ways."*

Here's an example of a balanced equation built around tangible value.

Overachieve revenue goals by 15 percent while at the same time reducing operational expenses by as much as 10 percent.

See the difference? The second equation tells both sides of the story and eliminates any prejudgment problems. With the first appeal, on the other hand, we are "shot down" almost before the CEO finishes processing the information. The person we're appealing to can tell we aren't thinking like a chief executive.

Now let's take a look at an *intangible* reward equation that's balanced.

Enhance employee morale and commitment while at the same time containing your benefit expenses.

You must master *both* tangible and intangible reward equations. When it comes to value, you've got to be ready to present more than one appeal. (You've also got to be willing to use more than one delivery approach.)

Add the Element of Time

Every CEO I've ever met lives in a time-compressed world.

CEOs evaluate *everything* by the critical element of time. How long will it take to realize a particular goal? How long will it take to bring a particular product into existence? How long do we have before a new piece of technology turns our market upside down?

This focus on time means that at the end of every equation you balance you *must* add the critical element of time. Here's our tangible, value-balanced reward equation with the element of time added.

> *Overachieve revenue goals by 15 percent while at the same time reducing operational expenses by as much as 10 percent—and do so in less than 120 days.*

Wow!

> Shorter is better! After you write the first draft of your balanced gain equation, see if you can remove 20 percent of the words you used.

Hot Button 2: Resolve CEO Fears

Believe it: CEOs get scared, too.

During my seminars, I ask salespeople to tell me what they think a CEO's fears are. I get answers like these:

- Buying something they don't need
- Paying too much for a product
- Making a mistake
- Succumbing to competitive pressures likely to affect their customer base and market share
- Mishandling labor disputes and production schedule shakeups

- Being unprepared for shifts in the economy as a whole
- Letting down shareholders
- Letting down employees
- Having to cut back head count
- Not being ready for change in the marketplace

You know what? These situations may cause concern, but they don't actually cause a capable CEO to experience fear. Most accomplished CEOs are ready, willing, and able to face *all* such potential headaches.

Here's what my experience with CEOs tells me they *truly* fear:

- Wasting precious time
- Being forced to take part in conversations on topics they know nothing about

My interviews with CEOs for this book confirmed my instinct about the pervasiveness of these two overriding fears. Note that these two fears are *almost always* associated with conversations CEOs are forced to take part in with (typical) salespeople. Note, too, that these fears are *rarely if ever* associated with discussions they have with other CEOs.

Which category would you rather occupy?

Fear of wasting time and fear of being forced to discuss things they don't know about are nearly universal concerns among the business world's CEOs.

Related turn-offs that CEOs shared with me include salespeople who:

- pretend to know them when they don't.
- ask stupid questions.
- ask questions that put the CEO on the spot.
- don't know anything about their business.
- don't have a clue about their organization.
- ramble on and don't stay on topic.
- have no or little integrity.

- don't know the value of what they offer.
- don't ask relevant questions.
- pay false flattery.
- try (in vain) to use icebreakers to reduce "tension" in a sales call. Who's tense, anyway? Not the CEO!
- show up late for an appointment (and thus waste precious time).
- exaggerate.
- automatically assume personal rapport.
- talk down their competition.
- procrastinate.
- tell lies.

> CEOs don't ignore fear—they go out of their way to learn about what brought it into existence, then find a way to translate fear into excitement.

Let me suggest that you read and reread the above list of "turn-offs" carefully before proceeding with this book. Note that it is based directly on information that CEOs gave me during interviews. The same items showed up again and again, regardless of the region or industry of the CEO I was talking to.

Model yourself after the CEO who sells. Make it clear to your prospect that you **will not** waste his or her time and that you **are not** hoping to show him or her up.

Let's look at each of these overriding fears independently.

The Fear of Wasting Time

Time is the most important resource at any CEO's disposal. When it's invested wisely, the CEO solves lots of problems and makes measurable progress toward goals. When time is wasted, the CEO loses ground and is likely to change physical and emotional states in a way that makes other people wish they had called in sick to work. CEOs will do virtually *anything* to avoid being placed in a situation in which they have no choice but to waste time.

This fear of wasting time is so strong that top officers go out and hire people whose sole job is to help make sure that unproductive squandering of the boss's time never, ever happens. These people, of course, are called "gatekeepers," and, despite the popular misconception, they are extremely powerful. These are the folks who have been given the duty of making every conceivable attempt to protect (and in some cases even manage) the CEO's time. They may know more about the business than anyone else in the organization (sometimes even the CEO themselves). They just know how to work efficiently without broadcasting that fact. This relates to fear number 2.

The Fear of Being Drawn into Discussions about Things They Don't Understand

Being well-informed keeps the CEO and other top officers out of hot water. It's one of their duties: knowing the trends and facts that may affect the business. They will rarely, if ever, willingly engage in or initiate a topic of discussion that displays their ignorance. As for getting them to come clean and actually admit to sharing with the rest of the human race the occasional act of being clueless, forget it.

> In order to sell like a CEO, you must commit to a campaign of constant self-improvement.

During a phone call, you'll know when you get close to a top officer's uncomfortable zone when she or he says, "I've got people on my staff that look into these issues for me; here, let me connect you." At that point, the conversation is over. You can easily elicit this instant response by using unfamiliar words, phrases, buzzwords, or industry technobabble.

Hot Button 3: Get It All Down in Black and White

I've spent a good many years researching, developing, testing, and revising written correspondence that is used in an attempt to sell. Here's a simple one-line report of what I've learned from all this experience.

Correspondence doesn't sell. People do.

Correspondence, when written correctly and delivered in a way that ensures it gets opened, read, or viewed, may get the sender an appointment (over the telephone or in person), but correspondence will not and cannot sell. Bear this in mind as you read what follows.

When I ask CEOs what they look for in the written correspondence they receive, I always hear some variation on the same four things:

1. Make it a quick read.
2. Make it relevant to my current challenges and me.
3. Make it so I can understand it.
4. Make it easy for me to forward to someone else.

Make It a Quick Read

There is a big difference between making something short and making it a quick read. Plenty of short documents are just about impossible to read; plenty of long documents can pull CEOs into the text and keep them there. (If you're looking for a "high-percentage shot" for a piece of written correspondence, though, keeping the text to a single page probably isn't a bad idea.)

There are a couple of secrets I can share about how to make sure what you send to a CEO is a quick read.

First, have several entry points. Anything you send to a CEO (or anyone who thinks like a CEO) must have easy-to-identify visual entry points. I am not suggesting that you use eye-catching

> Avoid, at all costs, words and phrases that challenge the CEO's ego. For instance: "Let me tell you," "Did you know…," "Here's what I think…," or "What you should do is…." Also off-limits: any technical terminology the CEO won't understand.

colors or "boxes" around your text. What my interviews with CEOs and personal experience have revealed though, is that you *must* use a series of headlines to catch the CEO's attention.

Think about it. What do you look for when you pick up the newspaper? (OK, after the funny pages and sports page.) If you're like most of us, you look for a headline that captures your attention, then jump into the article. When you're done, or when your interest in the article fades, you scan the pages for the next headline that captures your attention.

> CEOs will forward almost everything they read on to someone else, so make sure you put your name, return phone number, and e-mail address on every page.

Imagine picking up a newspaper without headlines. You wouldn't spend the entire day reading each and every column on every page, and neither would a CEO. You're both too busy for that. Yet the vast majority of salespeople I've met write letters to CEOs that feature nothing but text, with no headlines to summarize key points.

Use headlines. You should also use a secondary font, bolding, and italicized print and bullets to let the CEO reader know exactly where the key points start and stop. It's a bit of a balancing act, of course—you don't want your document to be so busy that it's unintelligible—but your product or service is worth it.

Make It Relevant to the CEO's Current Challenges

Most salespeople are brainwashed with product knowledge. Guess what? CEOs don't give a hoot about products or how much you know about them. What they care about are the *results* your products are capable of delivering. So focus on that. Build up an arsenal of success stories from current customers, and do the best research you can to point the right story at the right CEO.

CEOs will listen to you if you give them information:

- relevant to the attainment of the CEO's specific goals and plans during a *specific time period.*

- about how your organization can add value in shortening your prospect's time to realizing some aspect of item number 1.
- if you have it, about precisely how you accomplished something similar for someone else in your prospect's niche.

If you think this sounds difficult, you're right. However, it's not impossible. Take a look at this 28-word example.

> *Your 2003 goal is to grow revenue by 25 percent while cutting nonvalue expense. Our team accomplished that in six months for three of the top ten ad agencies.*

Note: It's best, at the very beginning of the relationship, *not* to mention the names of the clients or customers you've helped in the past. Why? By withholding the names, you focus on the results. You also give the CEO something to ask about—or boast about having predicted—during a later conversation.

The aim is to make your material *so* relevant to the CEO's world that the instant response is something like, "Wow! What results! I wonder how they pulled that off." Bingo! You just won the appointment-getting jackpot.

"Choose your words carefully" department: Look at the CEO's annual report—and "cut and paste" words and phrases that the CEO has used.

Suppose you have no existing customers to build such a statement around. Suppose you or your company is just starting out. What do you do? Here's one approach: Appeal to the "early adopter" mentality and present your idea as a cutting-edge solution that is so new that no one else in the CEO's industry has taken advantage of it yet.

Make Sure the CEO Can Understand It

If you want a quick lesson in the kind of vocabulary you should use in your correspondence, pick up a copy of *The Wall Street*

Journal and a copy of your local business journal. Sit in a quiet corner with a yellow highlighter and carefully read for an hour or so. Highlight every word or sentence that is applicable to the *results* that your products, services, and solutions have a track record of delivering or that you forecast them delivering. When you're done, show your artwork to three very important individuals:

- Your vice president of marketing
- Your chief executive officer
- Your very best customer's chief executive officer

Get their input, then compile a list of industry-specific words and phrases. *Build your messages around these terms.*

Make It So the CEO Can Forward It to Someone Else

It frequently happens that the head of the organization makes promises that someone else—or an army of someone elses—must work long and hard to keep. Each and every piece of correspondence you send must be written with the knowledge that the document *will travel.* You can, and should, suggest the preferred destination by name and title.

> Many CEOs have a strong "early adopter" mentality.

We've already established that the CEO is the ultimate "approver" of all-important decisions in the organization, including the decision to use what you have to offer. That said, we have to acknowledge that the CEO will, from time to time, "empower" certain individuals to evaluate ideas and offer their recommendations for a decision. You must know the names and titles of these individuals.

In my world, these individuals have titles like vice president of sales, vice president of marketing, and chief performance officer. That means I must find out the names of each of these important players and suggest in my correspondence that the CEO relay material to the appropriate people. There's an advantage to working this way. No CEO is going to send any-thing to anyone on the team without first looking at it.

Hot Button 4: Make a Great First Impression

There are five great ways to get your initial message across to a CEO.

1. First-class mail
2. Courier
3. Fax
4. E-mail
5. E-presentations

First-Class Mail

This is the most cost-effective way to get your correspondence placed on a CEO's desk. (A side note: I still don't know how the U.S. Postal Service can move my letter across the country for what seems to be a small fraction of what it should cost. Do you?)

Whenever you use this delivery method, I suggest that your envelope be a large, catalog-sized plain white one. *Don't* display your company logo on the outside. As proud of it as you and your graphics department may be, logos may cause prejudgment as to what the contents say.

Courier

This is certainly one of the more expensive methods for getting your message across, but it is fast and impressive if done correctly.

Doing it correctly can be more difficult than it sounds. Not too long ago, I was beginning work with an account and decided to use a popular courier to deliver my message. When it came back as "declined," I was confused, to say the least. I picked up the phone to call the CEO, and as luck would have it, he picked up

> Before you contact any CEO, try to find out whether she or he is sitting on the board of directors of one of your customers, competitors, or suppliers. Remember: Loyalty runs deep within the ranks of "C" level individuals.

his own line. The response to my inquiry about the returned packet still rings in my ears. "You should have done your homework, young man. You used a carrier that is one of my major competitors!" I was puzzled because the CEO's company seemed to have nothing to do with air freight.

As it turned out, the CEO I'd sent the letter to was a founding board member of *another freight and overnight letter carrier.* Was this CEO too sensitive? I think not. The incident demonstrated how importantly loyalty is to CEOs and how critical research can be to those who want to sell to them.

Faxing

I personally prefer this method of sending correspondence. It gets to its destination almost instantly, usually looks crisp and sharp, and carries a sense of urgency.

Don't use a cover sheet that shows your company logo; again, you must guard against preconceptions. I recommend using a copy of your envelope as the "cover sheet." Where your postage would normally go write the words: "please hand deliver."

Always call the recipient of your faxed correspondence to make sure it has arrived. (It never ceases to amaze me how many faxes are misplaced by support staff.)

E-Mail

Here are a few good headings you can use to get your e-mail opened.

- "Message from our CEO, Catherine Jones"
- "Overachievement of your mission statement"
- "Raise revenue while lowering expenses" (or any other relevant result or goal that's on this CEO's priority list)

- "Message for your vice president of sales"
- "Our telephone conversation on Thursday, November 9 at 2:30 EST"

As with a fax, the fact that you sent it doesn't mean the recipient actually got or read it. The rule of thumb is to always call afterward to follow up and confirm receipt.

> Don't assume that a CEO will open his or her own e-mail. Many CEOs are technologically illiterate.

E-Presentations
This exciting medium merges the advantages of audio and presentation slides. Here's how it works. You create no more than three slides with no more than ten words on each one. You create an audio script that is conversational and has a talk time of ten seconds or less for each slide. (I know these are tight time requirements, but keep in mind who is going to be on the receiving end of this correspondence.)

If you're not the CEO of your organization, ask your CEO to record the audio. Suddenly, you've got the best initial CEO-to-CEO outreach strategy there ever was. Who's not going to listen to that presentation?

Secrets of VITO

THINK

People who run successful companies make a habit of finding out about the upside and downside of any business opportunity. A balanced reward equation will instantly earn top-of-mind awareness from any CEO who encounters it.

If your balanced reward equation includes any of the following elements, you'll earn a spot on the CEO's calendar:

➤ Return on assets (ROA)
➤ Return on sales (ROS)
➤ Return on knowledge (ROK)
➤ Net working capital (NWC)
➤ Shareholder value

Don't forget! Always add the element of time when formulating your balanced reward equation.

SELL

You must take proactive steps initially and throughout your entire sales process to remove the two most prominent fears CEOs have about getting directly involved in the buying process.

Wasting precious time. (Time is a CEO's most critical resource. Everything else can be leased or purchased.)

Being engaged in conversations that include unfamiliar topics. (Whenever this happens, it's a direct challenge to the CEO's ego, power, control, and authority.)

When you get ready to develop any form of written correspondence for a CEO, make sure that you follow these rules:

➤ Make it a quick read.
➤ Make it relevant to the CEO's current challenges.
➤ Make sure the CEO can easily understand it.
➤ Make it so the CEO can forward it to someone else.

TAKE ACTION

For additional information and worksheets on:

➤ Written correspondence
  – letters
  – e-mail

– fax broadcasting

– e-presentations using the World Wide Web

Visit www.CEOsellingtips.com
Click on: "Get Info"
Locate and download Chapter 5.

6

*"In the end, all business operations can be reduced
to three words: people, products, and profits.*

—LEE IACOCCA

BUSINESS RAPPORT

You've sent along the perfect fax, e-mail, e-presentation, or letter (or perhaps a combination of all three). You're *almost* ready to make an initial call to the CEO yourself. But before you try that high-degree-of-difficulty maneuver, consider the lessons on rapport building that appear in this chapter.

A GIFT FROM A CEO

Early in my sales career, I was given a precious gift from a CEO, one that made a profound and positive impact on my selling style and career as a whole.

He hung up on me.

Let me explain. I had ten prospecting calls to make that day, and until I punched that fateful call onto the keypad, I had talked to three assistants, left five messages with receptionists, and resigned myself to one impossible-to-rectify wrong number. As I punched in the last number of the day, I thought to myself, 'What a disappointment this day has been.' That was mistake number one—though I certainly didn't know it at the time.

I slouched in my chair and listened to the phone ring. On the second ring, someone picked up and barked out the words, "Charlie Leland."

I had actually gotten a CEO on the line. I choked up completely. My mouth suddenly became cotton-dry. I almost lost my grip on the telephone handset. I stammered out the words, "This is Tony Parinello with Hewlett-Packard." There was a little pause I was apparently supposed to fill, so I asked what seemed to me a perfectly reasonable question: "Do you have a minute?"

Charlie shot back instantly, "What do you want?"

"Well," I explained, "Hewlett-Packard has a new computer system that's called the 21MX. It's the fastest on the market, with a whopping 64 kilobytes of memory. It's configured with our high-capacity disc-drive system and double-track magnetic backup. I'd like to ask you a few questions about your company. Would tomorrow at 9 o'clock be good, or would Wednesday at 2 o'clock be better?"

What a snappy way to get the appointment (or so I thought).

Charlie's response put me in my place. It was short and sweet. "I don't have time for this," Charlie said. Then his phone said, "Click."

For a moment, I was too stunned to speak. This really *was* a lousy day, after all. I scanned my surroundings to see whether or not anyone had heard the deathly silence that followed my request for Charlie's time. Fortunately, no one had.

As I drove home in my company car and pondered my brief conversation with Charlie, I found myself repeating a quiet mantra to myself, a mantra that proved remarkably persistent and served as the starting point for a deep two-month slump in my career at Hewlett-Packard. The mantra ran as follows: "I am a klutz...I am a klutz...I am a klutz...."

> Successful CEOs rarely, if ever, make the same mistake twice. Virtually every mistake is turned into an effective learning experience.

I thought about that call for weeks. Eventually, I concluded there was an important lesson to be learned from my short discussion with Charlie. When I'd asked him, "Do you have a minute?" I'd become one of a hundred *supplicants* begging for a chunk of his day without offering anything meaningful in return. When I'd launched into a discussion of my product's features, I'd proved for certain that I was yet another person interested in *wasting his time*. When I'd tried to force him into an "either-or" choice for meeting me in person, I'd shown only my ineptitude and lack of sensitivity to the demands on his time and the importance of his position.

In short, I had failed to establish the right business rapport with Charlie. By focusing in a self-centered way on what I knew and the unreasonable goal of setting the first appointment, I had made that first appointment impossible.

Once I figured out what had gone wrong, I never made the same mistake again. I never would have course-corrected though, if I hadn't spent two awful months pondering that horrific hang-up.

SETTING THE CORRECT EXPECTATIONS
FOR YOUR FIRST CALL

I've spent the better part of my adult life teaching salespeople how to set appointments with CEOs and other top decision-makers. Here comes the first and most important rule for doing so.

Never try to force the appointment down your target CEO's throat.

The aim of your initial call must, instead, be to establish EBS. (You remember how important EBS is, right?) So here's a promise:

You'll only be able to establish EBS if you can build the right business rapport quickly. If there's no rapport, *there will be no first meeting or first sale!*

Art or Science?

Some people say that building business rapport is an art, not an exact science, that it requires a vague and impossible-to-teach capacity to "feel the vibes" that the other person is sending. I disagree. Over the years, I've discovered that the ability to build business rapport is a process that is repeatable, and that, with a little practice, even people who aren't particularly good at reading the emotions of others can do it.

Contrary to popular belief, building rapport does not require that you appear to be like someone so that he or she will like you. My experience is that building business rapport has nothing to do with that. Instead, it is all about doing what most successful CEOs do naturally: show their authentic self while demonstrating the business value they bring to the table.

> Business rapport happens naturally when you put the CEO's needs first.

Do yourself and your sales career a favor. Post that principle in your office or cubicle, where you can see it every hour of every business day. Here it is again:

> *Building business rapport is all about doing what most successful CEOs do naturally: showing their authentic self while demonstrating the business value they bring to the table.*

That's the big idea behind business rapport. Here are some prerequisites for turning that big idea into a reality.

Believe in and Love What You Do
Every single one of the CEOs I interviewed for this book showed deep love and intense emotional commitment to his or her career goals. Every single one.

When they spoke, it was with passion and a very deep belief in their vision, mission, and fellow team members. How did they develop this belief? First, they reached deep down inside and created a mission—a vision. Next, they developed an unshakable commitment to that cause, the kind of commitment that radiates instantly to everyone in the room. Finally, they *rewarded* individuals who saw their vision and took action to help bring it about.

Do you love what you do? Are you passionate about it? Do you have a strong belief in your vision and mission? If you have any doubt about the answer to these questions, you may be able from time to time to build business rapport with some individuals, but you will not be successful in *repeating* the process time and time again with CEOs.

Know When to Talk and When to Listen

In order to build business rapport, you'll need to master the skill of judgment. That means knowing when to talk, listen, and comment on what's being said and understood.

> CEOs prompt others to talk by using encouraging sounds and conversational phrases. For example: "Hmm," "Uh-huh," "I see," "Right," "That's interesting," "Tell me about it."

In other words, you'll need to know how to deliver an effective and meaningful monologue, when to stop talking, and how to make the transition to dialogue.

This is not as difficult as it may at first appear. Ask yourself what it takes for *you* to listen to what's being said. Does what the other person says have to be of interest to you? Does it have to be from a credible source? Does it need to pose an interesting and challenging question or thought? Does it have to stir your imagination? Does it have to elicit a response and give you the chance to express your opinion or immediate reaction?

If you're like most people, you answered "Yes" to all these questions. But in a business setting, you may put these conditions on hold when interacting with a colleague or superior. Guess what? *CEOs operate by these principles nearly all the time.*

What you say during the call must:

- *be of interest to* this *target CEO.* (Remember what CEOs fear most: wasting precious time and being forced into discussing unfamiliar topics.)

- *come from a credible source.* (Cite specific, verifiable results; quote real, live human beings who will back up what you say.)

- *pose an interesting and challenging question or thought.* (CEOs are more open than you might think to a challenge. When someone asks, "What would happen if you doubled your commission on sales that concluded in half the normal selling time?" they stop and ponder the consequences.)

- *stir the imagination.* Consider using questions to inspire interest and, eventually, commitment—for example: "Imagine cutting [$1 billion] from your fixed expenses between now and the end of the year."

- *elicit a response that gives the CEO the chance to express an immediate opinion or reaction.* (Remember, CEOs are big on exercising power, control, and authority. Let them. Needless to say, a question like, "Which time is better, Monday at 2 o'clock or Wednesday at 4 o'clock?" fails this test.)

Know How to Comment on What the CEO Says

Masters at building business rapport know the importance of an occasional "commentary" on what's been said. Don't confuse this with what's typically called "parroting," which is simply rephrasing the most recent words of the speaker. This ineffective communication approach will almost always result in curt "Yes" or "No" responses from the CEO and will undercut the building of business rapport.

> Whenever you're with a prospect CEO, aim to spend twice as much time listening as you spend talking.

Here's an example of what I mean. During an interview with Jim Amos, former CEO of Mail Boxes Etc., I heard this:

I have created a leadership council; it's made up of 12 key individuals I trust.

I could have made a typical "parroting" response, which would have sounded like this:

So—you count on your trusted council members.

A "commentary" response, on the other hand, one that would help me to build business rapport, would sound something like this:

That's fascinating. So what's the most difficult decision your council members have had to make so far?

Be Willing to Find Out What Motivates the Other Person

Over the years, I've read a ton of books on how to get and stay motivated, how to find out what motivates the buyer, how to get someone else motivated to do something that he or she normally wouldn't think of doing. After all is said and done, I find all this advice inevitably comes back to a simple fear/reward equation.

Here's a dialogue that illustrates how CEOs who sell find out what someone's motivation is (or isn't).

Prospect CEO: *We've got to expand our distribution into the European marketplace by the end of this fiscal year.*

Selling CEO: *Interesting. What's important to you personally about capturing the European marketplace?*

The response will tell you everything you need to know. If the prospect CEO responds with something like,

Well, if we don't move into that market, we'll be out of business by the end of the year, the motivation of this prospect CEO is fear-based. If, on the other hand, you hear,

> *When our competition sees our widgets being distributed in the European marketplace, they'll be stunned. Our product is superior and less expensive. It's just what that market needs, and we are going to give it to them,*

the motivation for this prospect CEO is reward-based.

Generally speaking, if you're trying to sell something to a person who is avoiding fear, it's best to make your offer simple and to the point with quick time to results. Make it easy to buy a "thin slice" of your solution that will fix the problem now. Then, later on, you can go for the upgrades and a more complete suite of your offer.

If the person you're trying to sell to is being motivated by a "reward," he or she will generally move more slowly and be more methodical. The prospect wants to be assured that what you're offering is best for him or her in the longer haul. Expect this CEO to look at the competition and make you jump through hoops to get the business.

Secrets of VITO

THINK

Every successful CEO has a deep-seated need to be in control of everything. That's why it's critically important that you never, ever try to force an in-person appointment down the CEO's throat. How, you may ask, will you actually get to meet and greet a target CEO? Here's the secret: Build business rapport effectively, and your target CEO will want to meet with you.

When you master the four prerequisites that follow, you'll be able to get the appointment without asking for it. Remember:

➤ *Believe in and love what you do.* Make sure you show your excitement in an appropriate way.

> *Know when to talk and when to listen.* Remember, CEOs love to talk—and they're not exactly the world's best listeners.

> *Know how to comment on what the CEO says.* Never play the role of a parrot.

> *Be willing to find out what motivates your target CEO.* Ask: "What's personally important to you about _____?"

Sell

Once you determine what's currently important to your target CEO, make sure that:

> all your communications and information comes from a credible source (for instance, your existing customer base in industries similar to the target CEO's). You pose interesting and challenging questions. (Stir the CEO's imagination.)

> you give your target CEO the chance to express his or her immediate opinion or reaction. (Count to ten after you ask a CEO a question. Wait to hear what comes back before you say another word.)

Take Action

> Write out your personal mission in 30 words or less. CEOs know where they're going—and so should you.

> Create an acronym for your name. Assign one positive adjective to each letter of your name—and then ask yourself how each one of those adjectives supports your mission as you've defined it. Finally, make sure that you show your strongest "adjectives" throughout the entire sales cycle.

Special note: Both of these steps are extremely critical and should not be skipped. Here's why: When it comes to building business rapport, the competitive difference will always come down to you—not price, delivery, configuration, features, or brand recognition.

7

MAKING THE FIRST CALL

Taking into account the truism that CEOs dislike receiving calls from salespeople just as much as salespeople dislike making them, our goal in this chapter is *to make the call sound like it's coming, not from a salesperson, but from a CEO who sells.* This is easier to do than it might at first appear. CEOs who sell and salespeople who don't particularly like making standard cold calls have a lot in common. Specifically, they both:

- tend to have very healthy egos.
- usually enjoy conversations that are brief, direct, and to the point.
- are usually supremely motivated. (In fact, the top achievers in both groups are beyond being motivated—they're driven.)

- are decisive.
- are bright—often in a way that transcends book learning.
- are willing to take risks.
- avoid getting into the details of anything.
- are usually extremely impatient.
- love to win—and hate to lose anything.
- don't mind rocking the boat to get things done.
- aim high, take extraordinary action, and ask questions later. (If someone's feathers get ruffled along the way, so be it.)

> Move beyond "calling scripts." CEOs hate them.

With all these points of commonality, is there a "script" that will guide you through an effective call with the CEO of your target company?

No. (Sorry about that.)

GUIDELINES FOR THE CALL

There is no script that will instantly turn a CEO into a prospect over the phone. There are, however, a series of *principles* and *operating guidelines* that will help you begin the relationship with EBS and win the initial business commitment you're after.

There's no "recipe" I can give you that will always work with the high-level official you're calling. Remain flexible in your thinking and use what follows as a template or road map—then apply the operating guidelines with intelligence and confidence.

Before we get to the operating principles that CEOs who sell use to connect with their own target CEOs, let's take a look at four questions you'll probably ask yourself about the calls you make.

1: How Do I Connect the Call to What I Did Earlier?

You sent an e-mail. You sent a fax. You sent a unique, eye-catching e-presentation. You mailed a great letter. Now you want to know how to make the follow-up call to the CEO you've targeted.

Guess what? CEOs who sell don't try to connect the call to *anything* that went before.

They know it doesn't matter whether they're following up on a correspondence that was sent or using this first telephone call as the initial contact. If the earlier message made an impact, great. If it didn't, no problem.

Follow their lead. Never, ever ask a CEO, "Did you get the letter I sent you?" Never, ever say, "I sent you an e-mail yesterday." Never, ever say, "I'm calling to follow up on the electronic presentation I sent you." If you say anything even vaguely like these remarks, you will leave your distracted contact one and only avenue of response. He or she will have to say something like, "No, what letter are you talking about?"

The only point you'll make is that the person who was to receive your letter has preliminary symptoms of a serious memory retention problem. That's not a great way to build EBS or effective business rapport.

Do what CEOS who sell do. Simply assume that no knowledge of you, your company, or why you happen to be calling has been previously established.

> Every sales activity that an effective CEO performs stands alone— and represents a complete thought and idea.

2: What's My Goal?

What would make your call to a CEO "successful"?

When you hang up from the call and run full speed into your vice president of sales' office, what would you want to be able

> When you call a CEO, make sure your "talk time" is never longer than 20 consecutive seconds. Remember, the person doing the talking has the power, control, and authority.

to tell him or her? That you got an in-person appointment with the CEO of Big Corporation next Tuesday morning? That the CEO of Big Corporation referred you to the person who is in charge of their new product launch—and all the budgets supporting it? That the CEO of Big Corporation is so excited about what you had to say that he or she asked you to overnight additional information on your latest and greatest ideas? That you just hammered the first "one-call" close of your sales career?

Actually, all these are wonderful *secondary* goals of your first telephone conversation with the target CEO. Let me share with you, though, the *actual* goal that is most likely to be on the agenda of a CEO who sells.

Get a favorable interruption as soon as you can.

CEOs who sell know how much *they* like to interrupt people. So they know that if they want to make *another* CEO feel in control, they *must* let that CEO interrupt. That's how the relationship has to start. *Every* CEO I interviewed for this book understood and validated this principle.

When CEOs interrupt you, their egos get fed. The first and most important goal of your telephone call to the CEO is simply to get a favorable interruption. After that happens, you'll probably start moving toward one of those exciting "secondary" goals without even meaning to.

3: How Do I Get Interrupted?

We'll get to that. Be patient.

4: What's My Plan?

You've reached your initial and most important goal—getting interrupted. Once that happens, what are you going to try to point the call toward? Here are some ideas for the "blueprint" your call may follow. Understand, however, what CEOs who sell understand—namely that *the CEO you are calling must control the call.* You, on the other hand, will have *influence* over the outcome of the call.

Over the years, I've cataloged what salespeople want to accomplish from a first call situation (over the telephone or in person) with a CEO or other top officer. During my interviews to create this book, I asked CEOs a similar question: What would *they* want to accomplish during an initial sales call? It amazed me how different their list was from salespeople's lists.

Salespeople are typically interested in finding out about things like company data and demographics, who's who in the target organization, what the current source of supply is, what's liked and disliked about it, and what the technical criteria for buying are. They also want to know about the decision-making process and the budget. These are just for starters.

> Before you pick up the telephone to call a CEO, ask yourself: "What can I say or do on this call that would make this CEO's day a memorable one?"

Here's the problem: *CEOs who sell know that other CEOs instantly shut down when you ask about such things.* So they don't ask. Instead, they focus on topics that hit their *own* hot buttons. If you follow their lead, you'll find that CEOs will either answer all those other questions for you or point you toward people who can.

So what *do* CEOs want to focus on? I asked dozens of CEOs what they would want to know during a first phone call to a CEO and what they would most want to discuss with a CEO they themselves called. Here's what came back:

- The target company's mission and vision
- The target CEO's *personal* criteria for selecting a business partner

- The timeline for working together if there turned out to be a good possibility of a business match

> A CEO's vision is like a landscape—it changes with the seasons. The most recently published version of the company's vision and mission statements may well have been changed by recent events.

Wow. Some difference, eh?

Identifying the CEO's responses in these areas constitutes your operating guidelines for discussions with target CEOs. They're as close as you're going to get to a script.

Let's look at each in turn.

Operating Guideline 1: Learn the Mission

Ask about the 50,000-foot view. Ask about the strategies, not the tactics.

The Secret that CEOs Who Sell Know

Other CEOs love to share their vision. When they speak about the future, you'll think that they are actually talking about the present. For them, this future reality exists. *Let them share that future with you.*

THE TRAP. Reading the annual report and "paraphrasing" the mission back to the CEO. What a waste of time. This person already knows what's in the annual report. *P.S.:* What was hot when the report was written may not be hot now. Things change—namely, the economy, the world, and the competition. Therefore, visions and missions are revised.

MY ADVICE. If you want to make CEOs feel they are in control of any conversation, get them to speak about the mission by asking questions like, "Where do you want to take your company's [new product development] area this [quarter]?" or "How do you personally see the [economy] challenging your vision?"

Operating Guideline 2: Learn the CEO's Criteria for Selecting a Business Partner

The Secret that CEOs Who Sell Know

If you want to sell at the highest level, you have to find out how your company's corporate ethics, policies, practices, and procedures align with the high-level approver's ethics, policies, practices and procedures. *CEOs care about the fabric that keeps their organization together, and they want to be absolutely sure their business partners are in sync with them.*

THE TRAP. Not sharing important and somewhat rigid terms and conditions of the sale at the beginning of the business relationship.

> Back away quickly if what you can offer doesn't match your target CEO's needs.

MY ADVICE. Ask directly what kind of ally the CEO is looking for in your area of interest and expertise. If the answer you hear leads you to believe there's a potential problem area, *bring it up yourself.* Don't wait for the CEO to do so.

Operating Guideline 3: Learn the CEO's Likely Timeline for Working with You

The Secret that CEOs Who Sell Know

Very early in the relationship, you have to be willing to ask something along the following lines: "Do you see any reason that you wouldn't do business with us?" Every CEO in the world hates to waste time on business relationships that are noncommittal, nonproductive, or nonrewarding. Here's the way they think: Why have a second meeting or suggest any course of action from anyone else in the organization if there is no serious intent? You have to think like that, too.

THE TRAP. Not asking because it seems premature or inappropriate to do so.

MY ADVICE. Take three deep breaths to get oxygen to all your brain cells and ask at some point during the very first call, "If we're able to exceed your expectations of a business partner, could you see yourself becoming one of our customers between now and the end of [the quarter, this month, this year]?"

Believe it or not, CEOs *love* hearing this kind of question on the first call. They want to move quickly through the buying and selling cycle, and such an up-front qualifying, first-call question shows them they're working with someone who will make it happen.

Didn't You Say Something Earlier about the Best Way to Get Interrupted?

Yep. But before you read the following paragraphs, keep in mind that what you're about to read is not the entire first conversation but rather a small portion of the first call, which I choose to call the opening monologue. Remember, this is what you use to accomplish your goal of getting interrupted as soon as possible.

Say Your Value Statement
EXISTING CUSTOMER CEO

> You: *In the past [three years], our team has helped your marketing department find more than 100,000 new prospects at a fraction of the cost we expected. We have a new idea for your sales department that could shorten time-to-readiness while lowering expenses.*

NEW TARGET CEO

> You: *We have a proven track record in your industry for reducing customer churn while at the same time increasing high-margin add-on business.*

If you were to say this to any successful CEO who has customers, you'd be very likely to get interrupted. You'd probably hear something like this:

> CEO: *Who is this—and how much add-on business can I expect?*

or

> CEO: *What did you say your name was—and how much can you reduce churn by?*

You've hit the jackpot! Answer the questions and let the CEO direct the conversation.

I cannot emphasize enough, however, that you *must let the CEO control the conversation.*

I am sure you understand the bottom line: Get to the point, and do so while presenting a balanced gain equation—the same one you developed for your letter, voice mail, or e-mail message.

In the (unlikely) event that no interruption takes place, you'll move swiftly to:

> Forget about standard advice for selling over the phone. Get interrupted and be yourself.

Issue a Call to Action

Arguably, the best call to action you'll ever suggest is one that relieves the CEO from any further investment of personal time and gives him or her the immediate opportunity to delegate to someone else if he or she so chooses. Therefore, after your "value statement," I suggest you influence the outcome of the call and say something like,

> You: *Ms. CEO, whom on your staff would you like me to discuss this idea with between now and the end of this business day?*

Alternatively, you might move for a personal connection with something like this:

You: *Mr. CEO, our other clients are able to realize similar results in [90] days or less. How would you suggest we proceed from this point?*

> CEOs spend their entire day telling people what to do. Make sure you give them plenty of opportunity to do the same to you.

In the first call-to-action statement, the CEO will always take the out and say something like:

I want you to call our vice president of marketing, Diane Durbin.

Talk about a power referral. Now you will use a tactic that will immediately earn you EBS and assist you in establishing business rapport with this CEO. You'll jump to the most important call objective of all, and you'll do so with the confidence of a CEO-to-CEO interaction and influence of the outcome of the call.

Ms. CEO, if your vice president of marketing, Diane Durbin, really likes what she sees and wants to move forward with a business relation-ship with my organization, could you see yourself becoming one of my customers between now and the end of [this quarter]?

Again, let the CEO control the call. Look for an opportunity to ask about this CEO's mission and how the CEO evaluates business partners in your area of interest and expertise.

Finally, here's the way I suggest you end your first interaction with a CEO, be it on the telephone or in person. As the conversation is winding down, say something like this:

Ms. CEO, it's been an honor to spend the past ten minutes with you. The next time we [meet/chat], I'd love for you to tell me all about:

- *the most challenging moments of building your company.*

- *the most rewarding moments of building your company.*
- *your most recent philanthropic endeavors.*
- *your personal involvement with your next new product.*
- *how your organization has been able to thrive in a down economy.*
- *how you thought of such a creative product line.*

Nine times out of ten, Ms. CEO will say, *"Why wait until we meet next? Let me give you the short version of the story…"* and now the call goes into overtime and ends on a very high personal note. Ms. CEO hangs up the telephone and says to herself or out loud, "What an interesting businessperson."

Don't obsess over what *you* want. Obsess over getting CEOs to interrupt you, interrogate you, and tell you what *they* want.

Remember, practice, practice, practice these guidelines—but under no circumstances should you memorize what you've written down in your script. Why? Because no matter how hard you try, you'll wind up sounding like you're reading it. That's death with a CEO.

Secrets of VITO

THINK

Every telephone call, voice mail message, or personal interaction you have with your target CEO must sound like it's coming from someone who thinks and sells like a CEO. It should *not* sound like it's coming from a salesperson. To make this work, start by modeling the following five traits (the foundation for these traits are probably already in place):

1. A healthy ego
2. A habit of being brief, direct, and to the point
3. A dislike of losing *anything*
4. A willingness (and even enjoyment) of rocking the boat to get things done
5. A tendency to aim high, take massive action, and ask questions later

SELL

No script will instantly turn your target CEO into a prospect over the phone, so don't try to write one. There are, however, several ways to ensure that what you say and do will have a good chance of soliciting a "tell me more" response. Namely:

> *Always connect the call to whatever you did earlier.* But don't ask stupid questions like, "Did you get the e-mail I sent you?" (The CEO won't remember.)
> *Get interrupted as soon as possible.* This is the first and most important goal of your call.
> *Ask questions that get you key information.* Before you end your call, make sure you learn this CEO's:
>   – current goals.
>   – criteria for selecting a business partner.
>   – timeline for working with you.

TAKE ACTION

Here are two important steps for you to take to make sure that your first telephone impression with the target CEO is the very best that it can be.

1. Find a colleague, sales manager, or other team member (perhaps your vice president of sales) who will work with you for

half an hour or so. Show him or her this chapter; role play a call together.

2. Don't memorize anything. Instead, internalize the key principles and ideas all your opening statements.

PART 3

GETTING THE BUSINESS

8

CEO RULES,
CEO NEEDS

S ome of the most advanced sales tactics I've ever seen showed
up during a weekend seminar given recently by two purposeful, motivated, passionate salespeople who truly know how
to build relationships with executives. These two pros are persuasive and relentlessly positive. Like millions of other professionals in their field, they get up every day and head out the door
with a firm sense of the value message they need to convey to
their prospects. And like millions of their colleagues, they don't
carry a briefcase, a business card, or any formal presentation
materials; in fact, they sometimes need help selecting and putting on their clothing. They're children—and the two seminar
leaders, Anthony and Nicholas, are my nephews. They truly are
masters at the art of enthusiastic persuasion and presentations.

Anthony and Nicholas wanted an hour of uninterrupted play-time from me. And they got it. How, exactly, did they get what they were after? By using two of the "golden rules" of CEOs that sell (I'll give you the other eight in a minute). Specifically, they followed rule number 1: *being honest about the situation*. They also repeatedly embraced rule number 9: *redefinition of the word "No."* They used a personal approach that allowed them to start off their "relationship" with a new "prospect" (me) by sending the correct initial authentic message: "We're going to have a blast together—you just watch!"

That, it turned out, was the message I needed to hear. It was a significant motivator for me to find a way to "work" with these two seasoned sales pros.

As you read about the ten golden rules of CEO selling, you'll find that Anthony and Nicholas came about as close as you can get when it comes to embracing a successful CEO selling style. I didn't have any choice—they needed to look at the world in the way that they did. And they needed to play. CEOs have needs, too.

THE TEN "GOLDEN RULES" OF MEETING AND SELLING TO THE CEO

As you read what follows, I suggest you ask yourself at the end of each one of the "golden rules" how closely you adhere to the meaning of the rule. Of course, you'll have to adapt each of your first meeting situations to each rule, but as you do this, you must keep the rule's integrity. Don't change the rule, just adapt how and when you use it.

> Unshakable trust, integrity, and honesty pave the way to successful business relationships.

Rule 1: CEOs Are Honest, Even When It Hurts

This is one of those rules you should carry (although it may not be easy) into your day-to-day interactions with everyone. Never, ever lie to a CEO or anyone else (including yourself). If you don't believe in what you're selling enough to tell the truth about it at all times, find something else to sell. CEOs can't afford to tell a lie. Why? Because there are too many ears listening to what they are saying. This includes stockholders, the media, employees, suppliers, customers, etc. CEOs know, and so should you, that problem accounts, just like problem relationships, are those that someone overpromised and underdelivered on. CEOs and those of us who sell to them must be totally ready, willing, and able to stand behind every word we write or that comes out of our mouths. If that means "walking" on a short-term opportunity today, so be it. You can always come back tomorrow. And when you do come back, you will be remembered as a person of integrity.

Rule 2: CEOs Touch People in a Special Way

CEOs who sell have a "signature" all their own. They create a look and feel that others identify with them that's as unique as the logo on their products. Here are two examples of salespeople who adopted an authentic signature way of selling that's memorable.

Nancy Allen: aka, the "Cookie" Lady

One Friday of each month, Nancy delivers homemade (in her kitchen) chocolate chip cookies to her best customers. Why? Because she wants to show her gratitude in a way that's remembered. If you ever want to see grown-ups fighting over a cookie, follow Nancy on her next Friday run.

Roxanne Deluca: "Lunch and Learn"

Twice a week—every Tuesday and Thursday—she makes three baskets and hand-delivers them to people she's called ahead to make a telephone "lunch date." (Would you turn down such an offer? Would you ever forget the person who went through such lengths for you?) She manages to schedule and conduct three meetings on these days—at 11:45, 12:15, and 12:45—which gives her prospects ample time to enjoy their lunches. You must be a top executive to receive one of her baskets, which are—you guessed it—handmade and red, the color of "prosperity."

Here are two ideas for you to consider.

1. *Always sign your business card.* Whenever you hand your business card to any CEO, always take the time to personalize it with your signature and a special slogan such as:

   - *"Here's to your continued success!"*
   - *"To greater results!"*
   - *"To a brighter and more beneficial future!"*

When you give your card to a CEO be prepared for him or her to say something like:

CEO: *"Why did you sign your card?"*

You: *"I personalize everything I do for my prospects and customers. Signing my card is one way of showing you I will put my personal commitment on everything I do for you and your organization."*

If this sounds awkward, it's only because these are my words, not yours.

2. *Give the CEO a pen.* Take the time and spend the money to get a nice (not a "knock-off") pen with your logo on it. This should cost you about $12. After you sign your business card, look at the pen in your hand and say,

   "Ms. [CEO], this is for you (handing her the pen). When it comes time for you to sign our first contract, please do me the favor of using this pen."

Don't be surprised if the CEO reciprocates by giving you one of their logo pens.

As time passes, don't forget to send this CEO a new cartridge. It's a great way to stay in touch, and the pen will serve as your silent sales assistant in your absence.

Always, I repeat, always send a ha
after each and every telephone and/c
CEO. If you should have a meeting
lings, then you will still send a tha
CEO. You may want to consider
like,

✗ *Thanks for having someo*
Casisa heading up your stuae...
She really has a firm understanding of w...
taking your company and how our solution may be
able to help.

Have thank-you notes with the postage in your
briefcase, glove compartment, desk, and home office
and send them the same day as your meeting.

yc...
most powerfu...
way of getting
a competitive
edge without
doing anything
to your prod-
uct or prices.

Rule 3: Know What You Want, and Keep It Simple and Straightforward

CEOs are incredibly simple in their approach. Every
single CEO I interviewed was able to quickly and
accurately articulate what they want from others.
Can you? Let's do a quick exercise. Use the space below to write
down what you want from the CEO of your largest prospect. You
can take as long as you want to complete this exercise, but you
cannot take more than 30 words to articulate it. Ready? *Go!*

_____

_____

_____

_____

_____

_____

_____

what I want from *my* prospect's CEO:

our opinion on how to use my proven ideas to increase the ze of your entry point orders, compress your sales cycle, and get add-on business from your existing customers.

Now, get in the habit of asking for it.

Keep It Simple and Straightforward
A true story for your edification:

I was working to sell a large computer system that, once installed, would have the ability to automate the company's entire manufacturing process. I had the president visit our office for a demonstration on one of the system's unique capabilities, its "relational database," which, as you can imagine, is very complex. The president was sitting shoulder-to-shoulder with my systems engineer, my manager stood behind them, and I sat off to one side. John started his demo, and as he went on and on, I noticed that the president was getting more and more confused about exactly what was taking place. How could I tell? He got more and more quiet. He stopped asking questions about 20 minutes into the demo.

We reached a point where John had to take a deep breath, and during that pause, the president looked at me and asked, "Tony, how much memory does this machine have?"

I think he asked me that because it was the only question he felt comfortable posing—and notice he didn't pose it to John, but to me. I looked at the president and said, "Grady, this machine will never forget anything you tell it." He smiled and said, "Finally—something I can understand!" Both the systems engineer and my manager looked extremely perturbed at my answer. After the demo ended, my manager called me into his office and read me the riot act. "We're a technology-driven organization. Whenever someone, especially the president of an organization, asks you a technical question, you will give a proper technical answer. Next time, don't be so cute."

A few months later, when I'd sold that system to the president, I went into my manager's office, slid the $265,000 purchase order right on his desk, and said, "This is for the machine that never forgets."

I love moments like that.

Rule 4: Show Your Feelings

How many times do you tell someone how you really feel? How many times when you take that step are your feelings acknowledged by the other person? CEOs who sell show their own feelings and respond to others' feelings, and they are always, I repeat, always, in the present moment and time. Most of us think that doing this takes too much time. Actually, you'll save a lot of time if you take the lead from the CEO, and here's why. If you take the time to make *every* interaction you have with *everyone* on your way to the CEO's office memorable, your return trip will be much easier. Your calls will be accepted, voice-mail messages returned, and ideas entertained. In other words, you'll get top-of-mind awareness. Making yourself and your interactions memorable isn't that hard. All you have to do is show your feelings in a sincere way *and* acknowledge the feelings of others in a sincere way.

Follow the CEO's lead! For instance:

How are you today? *"Oh, I'm fine. No, actually I just got word that my cholesterol level is dangerously high and I must go on a very restrictive diet."* What types of food must you avoid? *"Fried food, some dairy products, any types of snacks that have more than 4 percent fat for starters."* Sounds like you'll be eating pretty healthy. Maybe I should look at this diet.

After this conversation, you send the person a recipe book on low-fat cooking and sign it with a message that comes from your heart.

To your health! or *Here's to healthier eating!* or *Put this to the taste test!*

Rule 5: Say You're Sorry When You Mess Up

> Effective CEOs maintain lots of appropriate eye contact.

Too many salespeople (heck, too many *people*) seem to assume it's bad etiquette to admit having made a mistake. Nothing could be further from the truth. CEOs know the importance of taking personal responsibility, and so should you. That means saying and meaning those dreaded words, "I'm sorry" (or "I apologize," or "that's my fault/responsibility," or any appropriate variation) when something goes wrong or is about to go wrong. You, not anyone else, should be the person to deliver this message. Here's why: Someone else may have a different agenda from you. For example, let's say you've been doing business with Big Corporation for two years, but you've never met the CEO (I bet you've got a few Big Corporation's in your current customer base). Your product causes a production delay or some other big problem. If you allow someone else to get the word to the CEO, the message may not be as accurate as you want it to be. It may be burdened with other "baggage" that has been plaguing the production line. Make the call yourself. CEOs are the most forgiving people in the organization, and owning up to a problem is often a great way to improve your business relationship with them. Say, "Ms. [CEO], if your organization were to make a mistake similar to this one, how would you make it right with your customer?"

Rule 6: Look at People When You Talk to Them

About half the interviews I conducted for this book were done in person. In every case, the CEO always gave me a generous amount of eye contact. Why? Making appropriate (not invasive) eye contact is a necessary ingredient of effective listening. Besides, if you know what to look for, watching someone's eyes can tell you a lot about their feelings. Generally speaking, the right kind of eye contact demonstrates a sincere purpose. Suppose you're getting a consistent amount of eye contact during a conversation with a CEO—but when you ask, "<u>*Do you see any reason that you wouldn't do business with us?*</u>" that eye contact stops. Something's wrong. This is what I would call behavior that's "out of integrity." It could well be there is a reason this CEO does not want to share with you exactly what may be going on (mergers, acquisitions, buy-out, personal "bail-out," etc.) or may not be at liberty to discuss it with you. The opposite of this is also true. Watch your own eye contact when you give responses to questions.

The best way to get your eyes to match your words is to always speak the truth. Remember this maxim:

Eyes don't lie…words do.

Rule 7: Get Commitment Early On

I don't mean you should invent meaningless questions or statements designed solely to get buyers bobbing their heads up and down like mindless dashboard dolls. What I want you to notice is that CEOs will always get early "buy in" from anyone who is to perform a task or mission for them. It's a way of transferring ownership so responsibility is unquestionably with the other party.

Since this is a strong leadership and selling style of CEOs, you can rest assured that when you ask for commitment from them, they will understand exactly what you're doing and what part they are to play. CEOs understand that it's always good business to balance the responsibility so you as the selling organization don't get too far ahead of the commitments of the buying organization.

> Never move forward in your sales efforts if the other party hasn't put something at risk—namely, time, money, or verbal/written commitment.

"Mr. CEO, our organization will be investing more than $30,000 of presales expenses working with your evaluation team. If you were in my shoes, would you feel confident making the decision to move ahead?" Bold? Yes. But perfectly appropriate.

Rule 8: Ask and You Shall Receive

This rule is closely associated with rule number 7. Whenever you ask a CEO for anything, you will get something in return. It may not be exactly what you asked for, but you will get something. I've built a successful sales career on the simple belief that the more you ask and the sooner you do so, the more and sooner you will sell. Here's a shortlist of what you should make a habit of asking CEOs about:

- *Opinions and impressions.* "What are your thoughts so far?" "If you had to make up your mind right now, what would it be?" "Based on what you've heard/seen/experienced so far, would you become one of our customers?" "If you had to sell your organization on my ideas, how would you go about doing it?"
- *Ideas for improvement.* "What would you do if you were given the opportunity to make our ideas even better?" "How would you go about making our offer even more inviting to your organization?"
- *Other members of this CEO's team.* "Who else needs to take a look at our ideas?" "Who do you trust the most to give this initiative to?" "Who in your organization will have the responsibility for putting our ideas into action?"

Rule 9: Redefine the Word "No"

I have an ironclad policy about the word "no." I never accept, at face value, any interruption that contains the word. You shouldn't either. Instead, you should ask yourself, Exactly what is this person saying "no" to?

Consider this example. Government agencies, school districts, counties, states and municipalities, and certain not-for-profit organizations may be governed by strict laws and policies that say they must buy the lowest price provider of any service they are in search of. Of course, there are ways around these requirements, such as being the only provider of a particular service or a "sole-source" contract. But in most procurement activities, if you're not the lowest price provider, you don't make the shortlist. If you don't make the shortlist, you can't make the sale.

> CEO: *No, we can't do business with your organization. We've got to adhere to the governing board's policy of buying the lowest price provider, and your organization is, from what our research has shown, the highest price proposal we have. Thanks for your efforts, but...no thanks.*

> You: *Ms. CEO, would you please define "price" for me?*

This is a classic way to change the playing field and get this CEO to look at what the real *cost* of ownership is. For many years I sold (very successfully, I might add) the highest-priced computer systems into the "lowest-price situations" by using this response to the word "no."

Rule 10: Issue a Call to Action Before the Discussion Ends

This is the part of the first meeting where the rubber meets the road. Some salespeople take a laid-back approach when it comes to specifying commitments. As you have learned, that's not the approach of a CEO. CEOs love the word "action." They constantly ask it of their own team, so you can also ask it of them.

The action I am referring to is one that puts everything in the proper order for the CEO. This means focusing on the steps

> Beware of responding to objections from the CEO with "Why" questions. These may well trigger an instant negative response from the CEO: "Because I said so, that's why!"

necessary for results to happen in this CEO's organization, not what *you* need to have happened to sell your stuff.

Mr. [CEO], typically what are the steps that have to happen in your organization to implement new ideas that have the potential to favorably impact your [take-to-market strategy] between now and the end of the [first quarter]?

Ms. [CEO], what steps did you take the last time you changed your [raw-material] supplier for your [Phoenix manufacturing facility]?

In the space below, write a call to action that fits your products, services, and solutions.

_____

_____

_____

_____

_____

_____

SPOTLIGHT ON THE CEO's HUMAN NEEDS

I would be remiss if I didn't reference the work of one of the world's most renowned psychologists, Abraham Maslow (1908–1970), who wanted to develop a thorough understanding of why and how human beings are motivated. Since CEOs are human beings, understanding and adapting Maslow's process to CEOs will be a powerful first step to understanding the proper timing of presenting your ideas to a CEO.

Maslow is remembered to this day for his highly influential "hierarchy of needs," also known as Maslow's pyramid. This is an ascending five-stage grouping of human "needs" categories.

Maslow held that human needs must be satisfied from the bottom or base of the pyramid, upward. As you see in the diagram below, Maslow placed physiological needs for a dependable environment (sleep, shelter, food, and water) at the base of the pyramid. At the next level are "safety and security" needs (protection of ourselves, loved ones, and possessions). At the next highest level, you'll find the need for "belonging and recognition" (family, professional, and social participation and recognition). The fourth of the five levels reflects the need for "social status, self-respect, and esteem granted from others" (a sense of value and rank within social systems). And at the very top of Maslow's pyramid is "self-actualization" (the experience of reaching one's full potential and experiencing life to the fullest). Take a minute to study the pyramid, then we'll apply it to the world of the CEO.

PHYSIOLOGICAL

Maslow: Dependable environment: sleep, shelter, food, and water.

CEO: Dependable environment: mergers, acquisitions, re-engineering, downsizing, labor issues, employee relations, company infrastructure.

SAFETY AND SECURITY

Maslow: Protection of ourselves, our loved ones, and our possessions.

CEO: Protection of customer base, economic fluctuations, stock valuation; security against competitive assaults on marketplace or market space.

BELONGING AND RECOGNITION

Maslow: Family, professional, and social participation and recognition.

CEO: Brand recognition, industry standing and relative ranking, customer service ratings.

SOCIAL STATUS

Maslow: Self-respect, and esteem from others, a sense of value and rank within social systems.

CEO: Leadership/creating followers, accomplishing vision and mission statements, teamwork and respect of team members, employee loyalty/retention.

SELF-ACTUALIZATION

Maslow: The experience of reaching one's full potential and experiencing life to the fullest.

CEO: Perks, expanding horizons, stock options, invitations to board seats, philanthropic endeavors, personal and professional growth experiences.

A Quick Exercise

Think of a particular prospect or existing account of yours, and write in the space provided what you think would be on the CEO's agenda in each of Maslow's categories.

PHYSIOLOGICAL

_____

_____
_____

SAFETY AND SECURITY

_____
_____
_____

BELONGING AND RECOGNITION

_____
_____

SOCIAL STATUS

_____
_____
_____

> CEOs are quick to engage in any dialogue that will give them the opportunity to self-actualize. Go out of your way to present them with such opportunities and ideas.

SELF-ACTUALIZATION

_____
_____
_____

Ratcheting Up

Here's the point: Maslow validated that human beings will always fulfill their needs *from the bottom*, or base, of this "needs pyramid" and move upward from there. If a lower-level need isn't satisfied, Maslow argued, people will focus on that need before they address a higher-level one. Take a look at the Maslow/CEO comparison chart on the previous page and answer the following questions, which are arranged in order of importance.

- Do you have any ideas that would help a CEO with mergers, acquisitions, re-engineering, downsizing, labor issues, and/or employee relations?

- Can your products, services, or solutions help eliminate or reduce the effect of: erosion of customer base, economic downturns, stock devaluation, or competitive assaults on marketplace or market space?
- Can you demonstrate your ability to improve or enhance: brand recognition, industry standing, and relative rankings?
- Can your product, service, or solution help a CEO create a better working environment and/or increase employee loyalty?
- Can you facilitate or add value to corporate perks, expanding horizons, stock options, invitations to board seats, philanthropic endeavors, and/or personal and professional growth experiences?

> Take your mind off selling your products, services, and solutions whenever you're getting ready to have a dialogue with a CEO. They only make investments that help them ratchet upwards on "Maslow's pyramid."

WHAT LEVEL DOES YOUR CEO OPERATE ON?

During your first meeting on the telephone or in person with the CEO, you are obliged to discover what level this CEO is at on Maslow's hierarchy of needs. For instance, if the person is engaged in a merger or acquisition (lowest-level need), and you're calling to obtain a substantial corporate contribution to your nonprofit cause (highest-level need), chances are you won't be effective in adding value to the CEO's day.

Do This Now

Expand your network (and your net worth) by finding someone in your circle of peers who can provide ideas, products, services, and solutions in all the levels that you don't. Work out a referral fee if you can and then refer your peers to the CEOs who have needs for lower-level satisfaction. After the need is met, return for a fresh approach with your ideas.

Secrets of VITO

THINK

Repeat to yourself:

"I am the CEO. These are my ten golden rules. I will use these principles every day in my sales work."

1. I will be honest, even when it hurts.
2. I will touch people in a special way with my ideas and insights.
3. I will keep my thoughts and ideas simple and straightforward.
4. I will show my positive emotions.
5. I will say I am sorry when I mess up.
6. I will look at people when I talk to them and when they talk to me.
7. I will always get a commitment that justifies spending my time early on.
8. I will ask directly for... (commitments, referrals, the "order," etc.)
9. I will not settle for the word "no."
10. I will always issue a call to action related to what I want to happen next in my sales process.

SELL AND TAKE ACTION

Sales work in general, and selling to successful CEOs in particular, requires that you pay close attention to the "hierarchy of needs" established by Abraham Maslow. Here's a two-step, fast-track approach to using Abe's ideas with CEOs.

Step One

With one of your target CEOs in mind, highlight one or more of the following initiatives that you believe to be on this person's list of goals for the next six months.

> *Dependable environment.* Mergers, acquisitions, re-engineering, downsizing, labor issues, employee relations.
> *Protection of customer base.* Economic downturns, stock valuation, competitive assaults on marketplace or their market space.

> *Brand recognition.* Industry standing and relative ranking, customer service ratings.
> *Leadership/creating followers.* Accomplishing vision and mission statements, teamwork and respect of team members, employee loyalty/turnover.
> *Perks.* Expanding horizons, stock options, invitations to board seats, philanthropic endeavors, personal and professional growth experiences.

Step Two

When you approach your target CEO, do so with ideas and solutions that address the initiatives you highlighted from the top of your list to the bottom. Here's why: Maslow validated that human beings will always fulfill their needs, and that forms the base of their "hierarchy of needs." As the need is met, move upward from there. If a lower-level need isn't satisfied, Maslow argued, people will focus on that need before they address a higher-level one.

For additional information and worksheets, visit:
www.CEOsellingtips.com
Click on: "Get Info"
Locate and download Chapter 8.

9

"I have often regretted my speech, never my silence."

—ANONYMOUS

MAKING A CEO
PRESENTATION

T he best CEOs, as we have seen, have a way of looking around corners that other people don't even know exist.

Specifically, CEOs look at the upside *and* downside of every decision they make. They perform a brief but revealing return-on-investment (ROI) calculation for each and every aspect of the sales process before they get involved with it. So should you.

One of the first questions you can expect from your CEO if you ask for their involvement in any sales activity is, *"What's the size of this deal?"* They want to know all the numbers that will be added to and deducted from the revenue your pending sale will generate.

> CEOs who sell think two steps ahead (at least).

You should want to know the same thing about any business deal you undertake. You should find out early, rather than late, in the game. And that's not all you should find out.

RISKS AND REWARDS

> Know the risks and the rewards of making your presentation.

What's the ultimate reward of a presentation to a CEO? In the short term, it's a single sale. In the long term, it's a series of sales. But you can't just look at the upside.

There are, at a minimum, three specific risks you will take in preparing and making a presentation to a CEO. Let's take a close look at each one so you can create your own balanced reward equation—just as a CEO would do—to evaluate the act of making a presentation to a prospect.

Financial Risk

How much do you think it costs your organization for you to deliver a presentation to a prospect? Good CEOs of selling organizations know the answer to that question. They have to. Why? Because presentations have a profound effect on the cost of sales, and that's an important part of profitability and/or shareholder value.

Start thinking like a CEO. Enter the number of hours and the hourly rate for each of the following four "direct" cost categories for any given presentation.

Category 1
Your time (in hours):_____ x hourly rate: $_____ = $_____

You're most likely not an "hourly" employee, so just take your last year's total earnings (base and commission plus any bonus) and divide that number by 2000, which is a rough estimate of the average number of working hours in a year.

Category 2

Technical support (in hours): _____ x hourly rate: $_____ = $_____

Will you require assistance from technical support personnel? Will they be required to do research for you so you can tailor your presentation? If so, estimate the number of hours they will be investing in this effort. While you're at it, give an estimate of the hourly rate involved. Your numbers don't have to be perfectly accurate, but they should be "in the ballpark."

Category 3

Administrative support (in hours): _____ x hourly rate: $_____ = $_____

Will you require assistance from administrative personnel? Will people be required to do research for you so you can tailor your presentation? If so, estimate the total cost of the hours invested in this effort.

Category 4

Management support (in hours): _____ x hourly rate: $_____ = $_____

Will you require assistance from your managers, sales leaders, or CEO? Here again, use the 2,000 hour rule-of-thumb. Will they be required to be present for all or part of your presentation? If so, estimate the total cost of the hours invested in this effort.

Write the total for all four categories line.

Total = $_____

Opportunity Risk

While you, your support personnel, and perhaps even your CEO are all preparing for and conducting this presentation, guess what? *You won't be doing anything else.*

That means other opportunities will not be being pursued during the hours, days, weeks, or months you spend on this presentation. I'm talking about the cold-prospecting call that you ignore, the follow-up call that may be delayed, or the existing customer touch point that doesn't get "touched" while you're preparing your "stellar presentation."

Successful CEOs know the importance of spending time on the right deals, and so should you. Here are two important questions you must ask your prospective CEO *before* you start committing anyone (including yourself) to spending time working on a presentation.

1. Ms. [CEO], what's likely to happen after our presentation if you like what you hear, see, and feel—if you're convinced that our ideas can help you overachieve in [X] area between now and [the end of the month/the end of the quarter/the end of this fiscal year]?

2. Ms. [CEO], what will you need from our side in order to be convinced we are the best choice to be your business partner?

> Be ready to ask what will happen next—and what the CEO will need from you—before you or anyone at your company invests major time in developing the presentation.

You read right—you must get answers to these questions *before* you or your team members spend any meaningful amount of time developing a presentation. You can ask these questions over the telephone, in person, via e-mail in the form of a written invitation, as part of an e-presentation, or through a voice-mail message, but you must get the answers. The answers, when combined with what follows in this chapter, will give you enough good information to ensure that you will never, ever be disappointed or surprised at the outcome of any presentation you give a CEO.

Political Risk

Internal politics can be poisonous to a sale. They can also make a sale happen.

Over the years I've developed my own system on how to determine "who's who" in the world of internal organizational politics. It's a simple system based on the fact that a) everyone has a boss and b) we are all influenced by the boss's actions and opinions.

Here's my system in one sentence:

Find out who is on the board of directors/advisors, then find out whom these people are loyal to.

Let's say for a minute that you're getting ready to give a presentation to the CEO at Big Corporation. You take my advice and find out who is on the company board. Much to your surprise (and horror), you find out that three of the five board members are customers of your biggest competitor.

> You cannot sell like a CEO if you don't ask the kinds of questions CEOs ask.

Step One

Before you invest any time and/or resources on your presentation, *you must* pick up the telephone, make an in-person visit, send an e-mail, write a note, or leave a voice-mail message for your target CEO. However you choose to get in touch, ask something like:

Will the fact that three of your five board members are customers of my largest competitor have any impact on your becoming a customer of mine?

Use what you learn about the board to pose a positive, direct, and meaningful question to your target CEO—a question that solicits this CEO's opinion and gets you the answer you need to put yourself in the best possible position.

> Find out where you stand before you invest your organization's time and energy.

Step Two

Regardless of what you find out in step one, you must find out how long the incumbent CEO has been in command and where she or he came from. Here's

> Learn as much as you can about what's going on in the relationship before you spend time and energy developing the presentation.

why. Suppose you find out the CEO you are targeting your presentation for came from an organization a few years ago that was one of your competitor's strongholds. Then you must also ask something like:

How much of an influence will your past experience with [NetCom] have on your decision to become a customer of mine?

Keep in mind that "best possible position" may not translate to "first place." Sometimes it's better to cut your losses than to continue to invest your time and your organization's funds and resources.

Suppose you are convinced you *should* invest in a given prospect and give a presentation to the CEO. What's your first step?

GETTING READY: HOW MUCH TIME TO SPEND

Each year I run a full marathon—all 26.2 miles. I've been doing this for the past 18 years.

With the exception of two of those 18 years, I've always run the same race: the Catalina Marathon on the Island of Catalina off the coast of Los Angeles. The other two years, I also ran the Pikes Peak Marathon. It's a run to the top and back down that big piece of granite in Colorado Springs, Colorado (the peak is 14,110 feet). These events are true tests of endurance, determination, and discipline. They require hours and hours of training. Typically, I start my formal training on a "base" level, and then, about three months before the date of the event, I run about 400 miles—*getting ready* to run 26.2 miles. That's a ratio of about 15 to 1.

> Follow the 15 to 1 rule.

I've found that running a marathon is very similar to getting ready to give a presentation to a CEO. First, you must start with a "base." Then you must apply the 15:1 ratio. For example, a 15-minute pitch will take you roughly 3 hours and 45 minutes of prep time.

GETTING READY: DISCOVERY AGREEMENTS
AND INVITATIONS

You'll start by preparing two documents:

1. A "discovery agreement"
2. An invitation

The discovery agreement is a proposed agenda that contains your understanding of the goals, plans, and objectives of the organization. It's a formal document you'll generate and send along with your invitation. I'll show you an example of one in a minute. For now, let's talk some more about the intent of the document and about what it *must not* contain.

The discovery agreement is a brief synopsis compiled in bullet points (CEOs love bullet points) that list your understanding of the unique challenges, initiatives, needs, goals, and plans now facing this CEO's organization. The discovery agreement is a hedge against incompetence (you're confirming the goals of the target CEO) and gives the CEO the opportunity to control and revise the selling process before it starts in earnest (you're asking for input directly from the target CEO).

> Use a discovery agreement.

Note that the discovery agreement *does not* explain or introduce your ideas. That's what your presentation will do later in the process.

Let me be absolutely clear on this point because it's extremely important. Your discovery agreement *must not:*

- reference your company's products, services, or solutions in any way.
- make any claims about what's right or wrong.
- make any suggestions.
- take any sides.
- be negative or judgmental about your competition (or anything else).

- reference any names or sources as to where you obtained the information.

Here's an example of what a discovery agreement might look like:

Discovery Agreement for ABC Corporation

World's Largest Widget Reconditioning Organization

Persons interviewed: James Collins, data management supervisor; Brenda Smith, VP/operations

Topics discovered:

- Accounting is currently experiencing payroll errors of 24 percent.
- Accounting has an accounts payable backlog of six weeks.
- Accounting has an accounts receivable backlog of 12 weeks.
- Human resource files detailing retirement fund availability is out of date.
- Human resource's implementation of 401(k) plan is now on hold.
- Human resource benefits program is in place but is in need of review.
- Human resource's state forms for government contractors need to be filed.

Discovery

Everyone in ABC Corporation who was interviewed is in favor of outsourcing the accounting and human resource functions stated above. ABC wants to maintain direct control and therefore will only entertain on-site services. ABC also has a need for temporary services in the manufacturing and process areas, but these are a lower priority. ABC is looking for a single source for all outsourcing needs.

PUTTING YOUR DISCOVERY AGREEMENT TO WORK

Before you start any meeting that's likely to conclude in a formal recommendation, you should hand each person a copy of the discovery agreement and ask the following question:

> *Ladies and gentlemen,* [pointing to your copy of the discovery agreement handout], *do you feel I've accurately described the current challenges in your* [manufacturing and help desk] *operations—or would you like to make any modifications before we begin?*

No matter what your audience says in response, you win. With a question like that, you'll either gain immediate acknowledgement and acceptance of your assessment, or you'll find out exactly where and how you've missed the mark. (If you've missed the mark completely, you can put your formal proposal aside and schedule a follow-up meeting to deliver your revised recommendation.)

> Let the CEO tinker with your discovery agreement.

Sometimes your audience will want to tinker with the wording. If the CEO in attendance is doing the tinkering, take careful notes and follow the lead of the tinkerer. If anyone else is doing the tinkering, be sure the suggestion is in the best interest of the group you're addressing by saying something like:

> *Is everyone in agreement that we should look further into Janet's suggestion to do [X]?*

Here again, you can't lose. If the answer is "yes," simply incorporate the changes and, if possible, address them as a sidebar discussion later in your presentation. If the answer is no, Janet can defend herself and her cause. As she does so, however, you *must not under any circumstances* participate in this decision or attempt to take sides. Your role is simply that of facilitator of the discussion.

An Invitation

Wednesday, May 14, 2002

9:00 to 10:00 AM

Westgate Hotel, Tuscany Suite

Hosted by: Parinello Incorporated

Topics of discussion:

Time-to-market compression

Marketplace expansion

Non-value expense cutting

Please R.S.V.P. by May 1, 2002

A. Parinello

760-765-1321 • vitoceo@aol.ws

The invitation is a personalized document that should accompany your discovery agreement (see the example above).

Make sure you get your invitation into the hands of the CEO's personal assistant at least one week *before* your scheduled presentation.

There are at least two reasons you want to get this into the hands of the assistant and *not* directly to the CEO. First, you'll need to demonstrate to the assistant that he or she is involved in your plans and thought processes. In other words, you want to make it clear from the get-go you will not in any way, shape, or form be trying to go over or around this all-important team player; you will never, under *any* circumstances, suggest your message is for the CEO's eyes only. The personal assistant *is* the CEO's eyes. Second, by involving the CEO's assistant, you'll score major points with the CEO because you'll demonstrate your understanding of how important the assistant really is and therefore distinguish yourself from most of the other salespeople the CEO comes in contact with.

THE AUDIENCE YOU'LL BE PRESENTING TO

Warning: CEOs are notorious for having key individuals "drop in" during presentations.

The vice president of marketing "just happens" to be walking by as you begin your presentation, or the CEO "just happens" to be wrapping up a meeting with the COO as you arrive for your presentation. ("You don't mind if Gail, my COO, sits in on your presentation, do you?")

Here are two suggestions for dealing with this situation:

> Be a facilitator—don't get bogged down in the target company's internal politics.

1. Think ahead, take the proactive approach, and in your invitation, suggest (by name and title) who should join in and when they should join in. Operative words here are: by *name* and *title*.

2. Think even further ahead, and take an even more proactive approach: Make sure you prepare handout material targeting, by name and title, everyone on this CEO's staff who could conceivably have an interest in what you'll be presenting. If someone "just happens" to drop in, that someone will feel welcomed and acknowledged. If the person doesn't show, you can give the material to the CEO at the conclusion of your presentation. (*Here, Ms. CEO— your VP of sales, Tom Miller, and your COO, Gail Storm, may find this material of interest.*)

In either case you'll look like a pro. (In the latter situation, don't be surprised if the CEO says, "Let me give them a call. Maybe you could spend a few minutes with them before you leave.") This is a good reason you may not want to schedule anything else on your calendar for one or two hours *after* your presentation end time.

ADAPTING TO LEARNING MODALITIES

> Understand the CEO's learning modalities.

Prior to your presentation, try to get a clue as to what your target CEO's learning modality is. This is extremely important.

There are three primary learning styles: visual ("seeing is believing"), auditory ("I hear what you're saying"), and kinesthetic ("I've got a good feeling about this"). Your target CEO will tend to favor one of these modalities. Delivering the "right" message in the wrong format is usually a fatal mistake when dealing with CEOs or anyone else.

So, long before the meeting, hook up with the CEO's assistant (you remember, that all-important team player you've included in all your discussions) and pose the question that may well determine the fate of your sale. Here it is:

> *Would you say Mr. Big prefers information he can see, information he can listen to, or something he can touch, such as a sample of our product or idea?*

Take a moment to commit that sentence to memory. Write it down somewhere. Practice delivering it out loud. Read it over once more for good luck.

If the answer is "information he or she can see," build your meeting around a sequence of visual displays. Back your visual displays up with detailed, written documentation, but *do not* attempt to recite these documents or summarize them with long speeches. Visual people are bored to tears by this. String together a bunch of cool images, and be ready to move from one to the next quickly. Use very few words on each of your slides.

If the answer is "information he or she can hear," build your meeting around verbal presentations, explanations, and responses. Your role will be to "hold forth" so the CEO can "take it all in," then follow up with requests for more information on specific areas of interest. *Do not* forget that you are doing so at the CEO's sufferance—encourage interruptions and redirect your presentation as often as seems appropriate.

> Be prepared to deliver to every learning modality—but know which one to emphasize.

If the answer is "information he or she can touch," try to build your meeting around *brief* statements and demonstrations (accompanied by passing around your product, if you can) that are followed immediately by question-and-answer periods solicited from the other individuals in attendance.

An important aside: You should be prepared to deliver *everything* you have in the way of promotional/informational material in *all three* of these formats.

More on Learning Modalities

Visual learners have certain easy-to-identify habits. They frequently use words that key into their preference for visual information. The CEOs I interviewed for this book who preferred visual stimulation made statements like:

- "I don't get the picture."
- "Get the picture?"
- "Can't you just see it?"
- "Here's my point of view on this...." (Don't be surprised if this CEO wants to sketch or doodle something for you; have two pads handy for such an opportunity, one with lines and one without. Always ask, *"Which one would you prefer?"* Nine times out of ten, the CEO will pick the one without the lines.
- "Why don't you just show me?"
- "Imagine this...."
- "That's brilliant!"
- And the all-time classic: "I have a vision."

Communicating with a CEO who has a strong visual preference can be fun because you can almost tell what's going on in this person's mind by watching his or her eyes.

Words like "brilliant," "flash," "show," and "see" are more likely to have a greater impact on a visual person than on people in the other two categories. Remember: If they can't see it, they won't believe it.

Auditory learners love to "listen" to the words being said and the way the entire message is being delivered. The auditory CEOs I interviewed for this book used words and phrases like:

- "Listen to this...."
- "Let me tell you...."
- "Let me ask you this...."
- "My question is...."
- "My opinion is...."
- "Tell me...."
- "I want you to hear from my vice president...."
- And the all-time classic: "Turn your ears on to this!"

Successful CEOs who have a strong auditory preference will be extremely sensitive to the pitch, tone, and volume of your voice. Never use a droning, monotone voice when speaking to an auditory learner. This is a bad idea in general but is the kiss of death when interacting with someone for whom speech and hearing are the primary channels for communication. Always modulate your voice and avoid any "singsong" style that incorporates only two or three vocal "notes." Pause—for a good two seconds or longer—when making an important point. Don't raise your volume when you're trying to make a point; instead, raise or lower the *pitch* of your voice.

Kinesthetic learners have an inherent need to get the "feel" of your message. They're usually *extremely* easy to spot. (I was able to identify this type of learner during my CEO interviews simply by the way people shook hands with me. It's very typical for the kinesthetic learner's handshake to be accompanied by a touch on the forearm; their handshake usually lasts longer than those of visual or auditory learners.) Kinesthetic learners really do like to touch, and they really do use phrases like:

- "That feels right."
- "That just doesn't feel right."
- "My gut feeling is…."
- "My sense is…."
- "I don't feel comfortable with…."
- "I haven't had much hands-on time with…."
- "How do you feel about…?"
- And the all-time classic: "I felt it in the tip of my toes."

> Know how to enter the CEO's physical space. It's trickier than you think.

Kinesthetic learners put a premium on emotional connection—feelings and person-to-person contact. They enjoy connecting on a "gut" level. Your challenge is to find a way to help this CEO *connect* on this visceral level with your ideas and strategies. Do not focus on the logic or external elements of the situations; focus on the relationship, on earning trust, and on the CEO's comfort level. Expect "digressions." Expect to be asked questions about your personal values and experience. Be as well-versed as you can about the challenges this CEO faces; show empathy and understanding to every such challenge that arises in the conversation.

Important note: In dealing with any business contact, we are always tempted to communicate by means of our own primary learning style. Unless you are certain you are dealing with someone who shares your learning modality, *overcompensate* in targeting your material to your contact's way of accessing information.

THE PRESENTATION: NUTS AND BOLTS

Customize the presentation to this audience. Make it unique.

Once you've got all the bases covered and the CEO has given his/her buy-in on what you've discovered, you're ready to deliver your presentation.

I am often asked by salespeople if it's "really necessary" to do a customized presentation for each and every new prospect. My answer is always the same: Either you *wing* the presentation or you *win* the presentation. I prefer the latter, and I hope you do, too.

Here's my five-step process to create a winning presentation for any CEO. (Note: I use the word "slide" in what follows as a generic label for anything that will be shown to your prospect CEO during your presentation. I prefer PowerPoint displays during presentations I make and listen to, and so do a lot of other people, including CEOs.)

Take What You Have and Make It Better

The best way to create a tailored presentation for a prospect CEO is to take whatever your organization has given you (I've seen as many as 87 slides) and make a hard copy of this material for your own review. You'll be editing this material down!

Now, take a colored highlighter and circle the most powerful 30 words that would appeal to *this* prospect CEO. Then create three slides with no more than ten words per/slide or *one* slide with a total of 30 words. It's your choice (I prefer the former). Forget the fancy graphic images or pictures of your founder in front of your corporate headquarters. What you're looking for here are 30 powerful words that will create equally powerful thoughts in the mind of *this* CEO.

Never show a prospect CEO the names of all your other customers. This popular "look how good we are" tactic only serves to inflate your own organization's ego. Instead, show only the logos of customers that meet the following criteria:

- Customers that are shared between your organization and this prospect CEO's organization
- Prospects of your organization and this prospect CEO's organization, clearly identified as "prospects"
- Suppliers to your organization and this prospect CEO's organization
- Names of individuals who sit on your organization's board who happen to sit on the board of directors of this prospect CEO's organization

> Highlight what you can do for this CEO at the beginning of your talk.

Always show any piece of financial data that aligns extremely closely to this prospect CEO's financial goals. For instance: The prospect CEO's annual report shows that her company is investing 15 percent of each revenue dollar into research and development, and you know that number is going to be increased to 20 percent for the current fiscal year. Your organization is currently investing 20 percent in research and development, up from 10 percent the prior year. *Highlight that parallel!*

Place the Last Slide First

One of the best tactics you'll ever use during a CEO presentation is to show your last slide first. In other words, show the balanced reward equation (see Chapter 5) first. Let's face it—nothing else really matters.

I know the folks down in the marketing department would like to think brand recognition and marketplace reputation are great ways to start the "education" process of your prospect CEO. But remember this simple fact and share it with the marketers in your organization:

> *CEOs don't give a hoot about who you are until they understand what you can do… for them!*

Your first slide should plant the value firmly in the CEO's mind. Here's an example:

```
Time-to-Revenue
Cut by 35%

Fixed Expenses Cut 15%

120 Days Time-to-Completion
```

Here's what you might say while the CEO looks at the slide onscreen or in the form of a handout.

Working with your team, we have uncovered a process to cut your time to revenue by 35 percent while at the same time containing fixed expenses by an additional 15 percent. Our teams have estimated a 120-day implementation, with a short six-month payback at your current level of widget production. In the next 15 minutes, we will discuss some of the requirements necessary to move forward toward these results.

Sell the way CEOs do: Hit the big vision first and leave how and why for later.

Note: Don't be surprised if the CEO stops your presentation at this point and says something like:

What's this going to cost me, and who needs to be involved?

Follow the CEO's lead. Answer the question and wait for the CEO to tell you what to do next. (When in doubt, repeat this presentation success mantra to yourself: "CEOs love to be in charge of things. CEOs love to be in charge of things. CEOs love to be in charge of things. CEOs love to be in charge of things.")

Proceed Backward

With only a few exceptions involving scientists, engineers, or inventors who have taken on the role of CEO, every corporate leader I've ever met works backward.

> Be ready for the CEO's question: "How much is it, and who on my team would you work with?"

Here's what I mean. These CEOs come up with the grand vision, mission, or strategic initiative first and then empower someone else (or a bunch of someone elses) with the task of figuring out the details of the tactical implementation. Mere mortals have a tendency to accept a task or mission as a given and focus first and foremost on the "how."

Assemble your presentation to match the way CEOs think. Start with the result and go backward—but never go too far. Never dive directly into the deepest complexities of your ideas; if you do, your presentation to the CEO will conclude instantly. Keep in mind that the CEOs you present to will not have (or desire) an understanding of how your stuff works. Don't try to give them an education about something they don't care about or have the time to pursue.

Remember the CEO's question from a moment ago? You'll need to prepare a slide that answers it directly. Here's the question once again and an example of how the principle of "working backward" should drive your presentation. (Notice that, up to this point, you've focused on "why" you and the CEO should work together first, not "how.")

CEO: *What's this going to cost me, and who needs to be involved?*

Slide #2:

> 9 Person Team
>
> $850,000.00 Investment
>
> 5% Possibility of Failure

Presentation (What You Say)

If you assign five production engineers, three materials managers, and your widget product manager for 120 days plus $850,000, our suspicion is that you'll be faced with less than a 5 percent risk factor to achieve the results we just mentioned.

Don't be surprised if the CEO stops your presentation and says something like:

How do we reduce the risk?

If you've got ideas on how to do that, you can explore them verbally with the CEO.

Stay Away from Your Product

Start with a benefit, just like we did in our first slide. Then, answer any questions that may come up, using an advantage just like we did with our second slide. Forget about the features of your product and service altogether. CEOs do not want to hear about the features of what you offer. As a general but reliable rule, they care only about the results when they expect them and the minimization of risks. So forget how your product works, along with all the parts and pieces it's made up of. (The only exception here, as I've already suggested, occurs when you're working with a CEO who has an extremely serious technical background and lots of time. If both situations are present, go for it.)

THE PRESENTATION: WRAPPING IT UP

When in doubt, ask, "What do you think we should do next?"

At this point, you may well get the response most salespeople would *dream* of hearing from a target company CEO:

> *Why don't you tell us what you think should happen next?*

I like to end my presentation to a prospect CEO with an invitation for my team (which includes me) and the CEO's team to move forward together—which means a thorough evaluation of my ideas.

> Ask what will happen next—and be ready with your own ideas in case the CEO asks about them.

Always place a value (a dollar figure answer to the question "How much will this all cost?") on this process, and include a timeline with a completion date that the CEO buys into.

Never ask a CEO, "Do you want me to keep you posted on our progress?" (If you do, you'll get this answer: "No, just work with my team.") Instead, send the CEO quick notes of your progress on your own initiative: "Met with the engineering feasibility team. Our study and schedule still on track." (E-mail or short e-presentations are ideal for this kind of update.)

Make sure whomever you're working with *knows* the CEO's desired schedule of completion. If, for example, the product manager can't seem to find the time to meet with you, and your third request for information and a meeting is met with no response, you can drop a note to the CEO. The note might say:

> *Your desired implementation date may be at risk. Waiting for product manager's response.*

Secrets of VITO

THINK

Why do CEOs take risks? Many a study has been performed on this topic. Most have concluded that by the time a CEO actually takes a risk, it's not a risk at all. By that point, it has been examined, calculated, and what-if-ed to death.

There are three distinct areas that a CEO will quantify before any risk is taken. You can start thinking like a CEO by asking yourself the following questions about risk:

1. *Financial risk.* How much do you think it costs your organization for you to make a sales call, generate a quote, and/or deliver a presentation to a prospect? Before you jump headfirst into a sales cycle with a questionable prospect, look at the associated costs.

2. *Opportunity risk.* While you, your support personnel, and perhaps even your CEO are conducting a sales call or preparing for a presentation, guess what? You won't be doing anything else. It's not easy to calculate lost opportunity, but it's important that you put some kind of price tag on your time away from the pursuit of business.

3. *Political risk.* Internal politics can be poisonous to a sale. They can also make a sale happen. Qualifying your prospects from the very top of the organization down is what this book is all about. (Qualifying at this level means you find out who's on the board of directors and what their loyalty is—and isn't.)

Before you progress to Chapter 10, make sure you perform the calculations on pages 108 and 109.

SELL

CEOs love to have everyone on the same page when it comes to a presentation. They demand everyone's top-of-mind awareness. If you want to sell like a CEO, you must think ahead.

Prepare and present a discovery agreement before you make your formal presentation. Get a buy-in before you launch a long, drawn-out sales cycle.

Let's be clear on what the discovery agreement *does not* explain or introduce:

➤ Your company's products, services, or solutions

➤ Any claims about what's right or wrong

➤ Any suggestions

➤ Any opinions

➤ Any negativity about your competition (or anything else)

➤ Any names or sources as to where you obtained the information

Let's be clear on what the discovery agreement *does* explain or introduce:

➤ An unbiased report of what you know about the target CEO's organization

TAKE ACTION

Commit to memory the following Ten Commandments for Delivering Presentations to a CEO:

1. Memorize the names of each of the individuals who will be attending the presentation, and use the name when you address the individual.
2. Always tailor each aspect of your presentation to your audience.
3. Always address the needs of your audience from the top down—CEO first, then all others in descending order of title.
4. Only use words and phrases that the CEO you are addressing understands.
5. Always prepare a discovery agreement and use it as outlined in this chapter.
6. Always rehearse your presentation before you actually give it to your prospect/customer.

7. Only conduct a presentation if it will move your sale forward.
8. Always choose the appropriate method of delivery (three-ring binder to electronic presentation), regardless of your personal preference.
9. Always prompt your audience to make comments and ask questions during your presentation.
10. Always finish your presentations on or ahead of time. (If "overtime" is necessary, it must only take place with the approval of the highest-ranking person in your audience.)

For additional information and worksheets, visit:
www.CEOsellingtips.com
Click on: "Get Info"
Locate and download Chapter 9.

10

*"The best way to have a good idea is
to have lots of ideas."*

LINUS PAULING

GETTING
THE BUSINESS

News flash: You can't expect CEOs to respond positively to any so-called "closing strategy." So don't try.

Attempting to "close" these individuals on anything is a total waste of time. So what, then, are you to do? *Open up* the business relationship, that's what—on the CEO's terms, of course.

OPENING THE BUSINESS RELATIONSHIP

Opening a business relationship starts at the very beginning of your interactions with a prospect CEO. It doesn't matter what method you use to create that beginning: U.S. mail, e-mail, e-presentations, a voice-mail message, a telephone discussion, an in-person visit, or any combination thereof. You must consider any and all of these interactions just as you would a job

> Individuals who crave approval from others tend to be the most unforgiving and critical. Successful CEOs don't crave approval from anyone—and are usually quite understanding when it comes to unintentional mistakes and short-term product/service mishaps.

interview—and that means you must let the hiring officer do the deciding.

Whenever you make contact with a CEO, you must be the best *you* that you can be. I'm not talking "perfect." I'm talking the real, authentic you. And when you're the best, authentic professional you can be, you'll make honest, unintentional mistakes and goof-ups. That's OK.

Here's why: CEOs know that no one is perfect; as we've seen, they're usually the most forgiving individuals in the organization. They have to be, because they have the highest standards of anyone in the organization. For most CEOs, the inevitable limitations of humanity have become a fact of life over the years. They're constantly pushing up against those limits; it's no surprise to CEOs that these performance barriers exist.

That's usually *not* the case with the individuals most salespeople are calling on and sell to. Typically, these worker bees get memorably beat up *whenever* they make mistakes and, not surprisingly, will do the same to any salesperson who comes their way. (Bear in mind, too, that most of the CEOs you'll come in contact with over the course of your career once earned their living as front-line salespeople.)

A True Story for Further Edification

Not so long ago, I sent an introduction letter to a CEO—I'll call him Mr. Jones. In my letter, I said I would be calling on Thursday the 21st at 9:30 AM. Well, much to my surprise, when I made that call, Mr. Jones picked up his own telephone. (It happens.) Fully expecting to hear his assistant Dorothy's voice, I found myself on autopilot.

I actually responded to his brisk "Jones here!" by saying "Dorothy?"

I knew in an instant I'd committed a huge *faux pas*. I was mortified. Having little else to say, I threw myself at my target CEO's mercy: "Oh, no! I just called you your assistant's name!"

Then Mr. Jones said something that I'll never forget: "I don't know who this is, but if calling me Dorothy is the worst thing you ever do to me, we'll be friends for life!" I then introduced myself, thanked him for excusing my error, and got back on track with the call. We eventually decided to meet in person, and he became a customer of mine.

What at first appeared to be a big, fat blunder on my part turned out to be a wonderful way of building business stature with this CEO. I am not suggesting you plant mistakes in your approach. What I am suggesting, however, is that you avoid getting all hung up on a desire to be "perfect" when you make contact with a CEO. It ain't gonna happen, and it's no crime to slip up every now and then.

> CEOs will move ahead and make a sales call to another CEO—even if they don't have all the information yet.

The Turning Point

If all CEOs knew just how much time was typically wasted by their sales teams in "jumping through hoops" for midlevel technical and managerial staff, they'd ask a simple question: "Why on Earth are we investing so much time and energy without a clear buying signal from the top?"

Actually, that's exactly the kind of question selling CEOs *do* ask on a regular basis, and when they don't get a good answer, they tend to call their counterparts within the buying organization. Talk about a turning point in the sale!

As I'm sure you must understand by now, if you want to sell like a CEO, you must make a habit of instituting that turning point in your own business relationships.

Tactics for Opening a Relationship

> Do what CEOs who sell do: Get commitment whenever you give commitment. Always ask your prospects and customers to move through the sales process with you. That means you'll have to get in the habit of stopping if they don't make some kind of commitment of time, energy, money, or attention.

As you take a look at the four opening tactics that follow (each of which emphasizes getting commitment at the *beginning* of the relationship rather than at the end of the sales process), remember that you can only use the ideas that follow when you're selling to a top officer. By "top officer" I mean CEOs, owners of companies, presidents, and the like. (Don't get too distracted by titles, though; think about functions. A law firm, for instance, may not have a CEO but rather a "senior partner" or "managing partner.")

If you try these ideas with *any* individual of lesser influence and authority, you'll run into a brick wall. Then again, if you focus your efforts on those lower-level folks, you won't really be selling like a CEO.

Put the ideas that follow to work with the right audience. Focus your efforts on the person who has the ultimate influence, the ability to change the minds of others, the ability to make independent determinations about how very large chunks of money will be spent, and who can instantly make any essential decision that affects the organization's well-being. Focus on the CEO level.

Tactic 1: Win Balanced Action Toward Commitment

If the relationship becomes imbalanced (that is, if you put in far more effort developing a proposal than the target organization does in evaluating the possibility of working together), your odds of opening the sale begin to drop very quickly. From a statistical point of view, it's best if both sides move *at roughly the same rate* toward a formal commitment.

How do you make that happen? Install these words in your first meaningful conversation with the CEO:

After our _____, I'll be asking you [your organization] to _____.

Here's what it might sound like when you use this phrase in real life:

After our first meeting, I'll be asking you to take a close look at our contract's terms and conditions.

Here's the rule of thumb: *Every time* you do something, I strongly suggest you ask directly that your prospect do something of equal or even greater value and/or effort. This way, both parties will be building equity and loyalty within the relationship at the same time.

Tactic 2: Highlight Critical Terms and Conditions of Your Agreement at the Outset of the Relationship

Always present your contract, terms, and conditions in a document that includes all the potentially challenging clauses; ask directly for the CEO's input. Ideally, you should do this in the very earliest stages of the relationship.

All too often, critically important contract issues are swept under the rug until the final steps of the "close." If these issues are potential deal-breakers, address them up front, at the *beginning* of the relationship.

Consider: There isn't a CEO in the business world who hasn't lost a big sale because of last-minute contract "issues." Most successful CEOs would love to have their salespeople presenting specific terms and conditions of the sale to each and every new prospect on the *first call* with the CEO.

If your prospect or customer is in a competitive marketplace, err on the side of conservatism when dropping names. Use a relative ranking: "the third largest law firm in southern New Jersey."

Take a copy of your standard terms and conditions with you on each and every initial sales call you make on the CEO. Provide the CEO with a yellow, logo-embossed (yours, of course) highlighter and ask the CEO to mark up anything he or she sees may cause a problem between the two organizations in the pursuit of a mutually beneficial business relationship.

Tactic 3: Ask Directly, "What Do You Think We Should Do Next?"

When in doubt, ask for instructions. CEOs love to issue orders. If for some reason you haven't gotten yours, issue this invitation:

What can your team do to assist in our next step?

or

What would you like to see our team do next?

Once again: You cannot close a CEO. You can, however, open up the relationship and move toward partnership in a balanced way.

THE ART OF NEGOTIATING LIKE A CEO

> Negotiating with a CEO? You'll be starting out at a disadvantage, but that's OK.

Generally speaking, CEOs like to play the role of negotiator. Most of them use their power, control, and authority as a major element of their negotiating approach.

Unless you have the title of CEO, you'll be starting off with a slight handicap. That's a given. What follows is intended primarily as an overview to give you an idea of what you'll be facing in the (very likely) event that a CEO starts "dictating" the terms of your new relationship.

Five Typical Areas of CEO "Give and Take"

Here are five elements CEOs love to bring into the negotiating process (forewarned is forearmed).

1. *Penalties/consequences* for late or poor performance on your organization's part. These
   may address delivery times, quality of the
   product or service delivered, or completion of
   projects on time and on budget.

> Do what CEOs
> do: Ask for
> something big.

2. *Payment terms, down payments, interest rates,
   lease rates, late payment charges,* or anything else that has to
   do with money.
3. *Aggressive delivery dates,* especially if what you're selling has
   to do with the most mission-critical strategic initiatives.
4. *Cost of ownership.* This is not to be confused with price.
   Cost includes lots of conditions that are not paid for
   and/or do not show up on an invoice.
5. *Service policies.* This includes such things as escalation
   policies, response times, and spare parts support.

Negotiating by Operating Style

You'll recall that in Chapter 3 I discussed the four business personality styles you'll most likely run into at the CEO level. Here
then is what you can expect when any one of these styles get
engaged with the negotiation process.

The Analytical CEO

These CEOs live to pick things apart, find flaws, and request new
data. When negotiating with someone who adopts an analytical
style, bear these points in mind:

- *Likely objective.* This CEO wants a black-and-white resolution to each and every point raised. The resolution should
  be both timely (being on time counts for a great deal) and
  thorough. So stick to the facts, don't skip any steps, and
  shine a spotlight on your in-depth research.
- *Likely tactics.* Expect an all-consuming focus on facts and
  figures. Expect a rigid, formal discussion of the decision-

making/approval process (akin to Robert's Rules of Order).

- *Possible Achilles heel.* The rigid, unemotional decision-making/approver style may lead this buyer to rely too heavily on logic. This buyer may cling to procedural points at the expense of other, more important questions. This negotiator is likely to be uncomfortable with, and perhaps ill-informed about, issues that can't be quantified.

- *Your approach.* Show proof for every statement you make. Use data, studies, or contracts from past experiences. Substantiate your case; supply as much written material as possible. Keep in mind that, unlike the amiable or expressive styles, the analytical CEO is unlikely to show outward emotion.

The Expressive CEO

These CEOs love to talk, talk, talk—preferably about themselves. When negotiating with someone who adopts an expressive style, bear these points in mind:

- *Likely objective.* These CEOs typically seek proof of their own influence, connections, and persuasive ability. They are likely to want to find a way for everyone to win. So make sure you respect the CEO's pronouncements and build your proposals around them.

- *Likely tactics.* Expect this CEO to be animated, disorganized, and highly opinionated. This buyer may try to gain points from you by saying, "Let me play the devil's advocate...."

- *Possible Achilles heel.* Susceptible to flattery. May be self-centered and a poor listener. Sometimes has great difficulty seeing anyone else's point of view. You'll gain influence if you accept this CEO's outlook as more or less divinely inspired.

- *Your approach.* Expressives love to win, especially while everyone is watching. Find a prominent way to give the CEO *something.* Where you can honestly and credibly do so, be prepared to use language like, "We don't normally do this," or "I've never seen my company make a concession on [spare parts support] quite like this."

> Know how the different personality types are likely to negotiate.

The Amiable CEO

Simply stated, these CEOs avoid conflict and dissension; they want to keep everyone happy. When negotiating with someone who adopts an amiable style, bear these points in mind:

- *Likely objective.* As a general rule, this CEO wants to do what's right for everyone and would prefer it if negotiations were unnecessary because everyone already agreed on everything. So help this CEO make the negotiating process simple, painless, and relatively quick. Keep things simple, and emphasize how happy what you're doing together will make everyone in both the buying and selling organization.

- *Likely tactics.* There may be no "tactics" as such. These CEOs may simply focus on the solution that ruffles the fewest feathers.

- *Possible Achilles heel.* These buyers are easily convinced and can (at least initially) be swayed to the thinking of others. Warning: If your company's negotiating team pushes these Amiable CEOs too hard, they'll call off all discussions and decide on nothing.

- *Your approach.* Keep it low-key. Negotiations must always sound like (and be) friendly conversations. Treat this person like a family member by making credible, honest appeals: "I personally care about your strategic initiatives, and I want you to know I'll be looking out for your interests as we go forward."

The Driver CEO

Stand back. The Driver CEOs, you'll remember, are the ones who get right to the point. When negotiating with someone who adopts a Driver style, bear these points in mind:

- *Likely objective.* One word: victory! Forget anything you may have read about "win-win" outcomes. In this CEO's world, only one person gets to win. Guess who it's going to be?

- *Likely tactics.* Intimidation, intense focus, and an overbearing attitude. Don't be surprised (or lose your composure) if this CEO issues mild, or veiled, threats. For that matter, don't be surprised to hear overt threats. Just keep them all in perspective.

- *Possible Achilles heel.* That hardheaded attitude may cost them. These CEOs have been known to dig in on a single issue and lose sight of just about everything else. The "all-or-nothing" approach has its limitations.

- *Your approach.* Hold on to your wallet and be prepared to take the heat. "Acceleration" is the word to remember here. You may be surprised at how quickly this CEO gets to the bottom-line position.

GUIDING PRINCIPLES OF POSITIONING

When you hear blanket statements like, "Your delivery date is totally unworkable" or "Your financial terms are unreasonable," ask yourself:

- *Do I know this individual CEO's style (Analytical, Amiable, Expressive, Driver)?* Is it too early in the conversation for me to be addressing this particular topic with this person? Should I really be the person addressing this particular topic? Is it possible the issue that's been raised is a "smokescreen" hiding some other topic/issue/loyalty?

- *What's my understanding of this CEO's organization's focus?* Is there a good reason for the pronouncement I just heard? In the case of a price objection, is the organization in an aggressive, cost-cutting mode? Remember: CEOs of buying organizations buy the way they sell (and vice versa).

- *What is this CEO's perspective?* For instance: Note that "too expensive" or "not fast enough" means very different things to different groups of people. Get in the habit of asking questions like, "How fast would you be able to use our ideas?"

- *Is this CEO serious or simply engaging in the ritualistic posturing many superiors require of those who conduct negotiations?*

> Don't present the target CEO with "special deals" or "act before the end of the month!" pressure tactics. They simply won't work.

MAKING GUARANTEES AND KEEPING AWAY FROM THE COURTHOUSE

Over the years I've seen many good intentions misunderstood and misinterpreted because someone used one or more of the following words and/or phrases:

- *"We guarantee it."*
- *"If it doesn't work, you'll get your entire investment back."*
- *"We'll promise…"*(delivery, quality, service response, etc.).
- *"I'll take care of it."*

We love to make guarantees; they can, in the right circumstances, provide a competitive edge. Lots of salespeople tell themselves guarantees work because they highlight positive aspects of the product or service under discussion. Actually, they work because they tend to make it appear to the buying organization

> Think twice
> before you
> make a
> guarantee.

that there's little or no risk involved in making the decision. Most of the time, that's a far cry from the truth.

If your organization does make guarantees, it's important to be accurate and honest when you explain them. Consider this example:

Our widgets are guaranteed. If you don't like what you see when they're installed on your production line, you'll get your entire investment back.

It sounds great, but is it accurate? You'd better find out. Will your organization really refund all monies if the customer doesn't like the way a single widget looks? And that phrase "entire investment" is a disaster waiting to happen. What if your customer had to modify the ventilation systems in six manufacturing facilities in order to accommodate your product? Would you be willing to bet that a hungry attorney wouldn't be able to convince someone, somewhere, that this expense should be included in the customer's "entire investment?"

The odds are that your company has spent a good deal of time and legal brainpower developing the language of your guarantee. Read it. And when you talk about the guarantee to the buying organization, avoid sweeping statements you can't back up. Stick with something like this:

Our widgets are guaranteed. Let me go over our policy with you when we're finished here and then I'll give you a copy of your own so you can review it.

A Word of Caution About the "G" Word

You should never *begin* a relationship with a buying organization's CEO by appealing to a guarantee. Period. That means you should not attempt to work the guarantee into your opening statement, either on the phone or in person. Appealing to a guarantee at this phase of the relationship is a sign of weakness, not strength.

What, the CEO is apt to be thinking, is that guarantee meant to compensate for?

If a CEO should ask about a guarantee, by all means give all the details.

In the early stages of my organization's development, I had a strong guarantee for my services. Nowadays, I still show the guarantee on my contracts, but the language is crossed out and initialed by my COO. When the buying organization sees it crossed out, I inevitably hear this question: "Why don't you offer this guarantee any longer?" Our response is, "Not one of our clients ever had to exercise it, so we no longer offer it."

As it turns out, this statement has had more impact than the guarantee ever did.

Keeping on the Right Side of the Law

I'm not a lawyer, and I don't know about the specifics of your selling environment, so I'm not going to pretend to be able to pass along advice about the legal ins and outs of your business. What I'm going to pass along is even better.

Below, you'll find my personal Eleven Commandments for Avoiding Legal Problems. If you follow this advice, you'll help your organization—and yourself—avoid the lawyers' offices and the courtroom. We've been talking about guarantees in this chapter, and I assume you already know that no one can guarantee you'll never run into problems with lawsuits. I can promise you one thing: If *you don't* adhere to all the steps in the following list, you'll end up regretting it someday soon. So review this list closely or, even better, make a photocopy for your personal use and post it where everyone (including your boss) can see it.

1. If you don't have the title of CEO and are asked to sign something, explain that you don't have the authority. Offer to hand deliver the document to your CEO and/or your legal counsel, then don't say another word.

2. If you don't have the title of CEO and you're asked to speak to any lawyers, politely decline. Lawyers live to start trouble. That's their version of prospecting for new business.

3. If you don't have the title of CEO, be sure you always follow the rules your organization has established for handling customer complaints. In other words, don't take on any assignments that aren't in your job title.

4. If you don't have the title of CEO, avoid making claims beyond the limits of your sales role. Resist the temptation when you're with a buying organization's CEO to pretend you can do something you can't. This approach always backfires.

5. If you don't have the title of CEO, don't try to rewrite your organization's policies or bend them in any way.

6. No matter what your title is, make sure you know about all the regulatory issues that affect your industry and the products, services, and solutions you sell.

7. No matter what your title is, make sure you know what your organization's policies are and precisely how they affect buying organizations.

8. No matter what your title is, put your prospects and customers first when they're right—and let them know tactfully when they're wrong, too.

9. No matter what your title is, do what you say you're going to do. If you can't do it or if you've never done it before, say so openly.

10. No matter what your title is, tell the truth. Honesty and integrity, as the old saying reminds us, have a distinct advantage over falsehood. The truth is always easier to remember.

11. Stay away from the words "I think." They have a way of getting you into trouble.

Secrets of VITO

THINK

If you want to think like a CEO you must reframe the word "close" and apply the rules for "opening" business relationships.

SELL

Immediately begin to use the following tactics to open deals rather than close them:

Tactic #1: Win Balanced Action Toward Commitment
Here's the rule of thumb: Every time you do something, you must ask your prospect to do something of equal or even greater value. This way both parties will be building equity and loyalty within the relationship bank account. Set the expectations of your target CEO by saying this:

After our _____ I'll be asking you (your organization) to _____ .

Tactic #2: Highlight Critical Terms and Conditions of Your Agreement at the Outset of the Relationship
During the earliest stages of the business relationship, present your contract, terms, and conditions in a document that includes potentially challenging clauses. Ask directly for the CEO's input.

Tactic #3: Ask Directly, "What Do You Think We Should Do Next?"
CEOs love to issue orders. If for some reason you haven't gotten yours, issue this invitation:

Which one of your team members—Joan Roberts, Alfred Russo, Phyllis Casisa, or Caroline Brewer—would you like me to continue this conversation with between now and the end of the business week?

Don't be surprised if you hear, "Let's do it right now!"

TAKE ACTION

When you follow the insights in the previous chapters of this book, you'll find that you'll be accelerating your sales process. You'll also find yourself at the negotiating table with your target CEO sooner than you'd expect. It's not too early to put the following negotiating guidelines and insights in your hip pocket.

> ➤ Do you know this individual CEO's style (Analytical, Amiable, Expressive, Driver)?
> ➤ What's your understanding of this CEO's organizational focus? (Remember: CEOs of buying organizations buy the way they sell, and vice versa.) What is this CEO's perspective?
> ➤ Is this CEO serious, or is he or she engaging in the ritualistic posturing that often accompanies any negotiating discussion?

Before you continue, review the Eleven Commandments for Avoiding Legal Problems with your manager/team.

PART 4

OPERATIONS

11

---

*"Define your business goals clearly so that others
can see them as you do."*

—J. PAUL GETTY

THE CEO SALES
PROCESS

Let's start this chapter with a truism. Each and every organization dedicated to making a profit produces something: automobiles, advice, cough medicine, computer chips, potato chips, whatever. And here's another truism: Whether the "something" that gets produced is as rigid as potato chips or as fluid as water, there are clear recipes, procedures, and processes that, when followed, will create a desired result for some customer or end user.

All those procedures move through an element called "time." That's a precious resource. It may well be the ultimate resource.

Countless studies have been made about how to increase the speed of various manufacturing steps so that a given outcome (that is, a product or service) can be produced with less expense and made available to the consumer with greater respect for that ultimate resource, time. In this chapter, we will discover how to apply a similar level of analysis in order to:

- identify every human element of the sales process.
- measure sales process time precisely.
- analyze the sales process.
- improve the sales process.
- control the sales process.
- replicate the sales process as a CEO would.

You'll find that CEOs who sell will *selectively* engage themselves in many of the steps we'll be discussing; however, the smartest CEOs who sell never take on practical responsibility for completing any one of these tasks.

IDENTIFY THE HUMAN ELEMENTS OF YOUR ORGANIZATION'S SALES PROCESS

> CEOs love to empower others—but they always know the buck stops with them.

CEOs don't treat all categories of potential business relationships equally, and neither should you. Your time, your organization's resources, and your revenue forecasts must reflect your interactions with various people in very different business relationship categories. Identifying (that is, understanding the elements of) your organization's sales process means identifying the various groups that make that process possible.

There are five groups you must understand in order to fully identify your organization's sales process.

1. *Suspects* are individuals or organizations who fit some pre-qualification filter or list of criteria, whether that's a profile developed by your marketing department or your own quantified set of criteria, which I call the template of the ideal prospect (TIP).

2. *Prospects* are those individuals or companies who have already been contacted by some method and who comply

with the criteria necessary to become customers, business partners, and/or distributors.

3. *Customers* currently buy from you. The key word here is "currently." Most salespeople have a fairly loose definition of a customer—some actually consider a customer to be "anyone I spoke to over the past six months about the possibility of working with us." All effective CEOs, however, know that a customer is someone who is providing contributions to the top line and doing so *right now*. Use this definition of a customer over any other.

4. *Business partners* not only buy from you currently but also prosper from their relationship with you in a way that clearly surpasses what your product, service, or solution does for them. That means, for instance, that you might share critical knowledge, strategic resources, leads, prospects, or even customers for mutually beneficial reasons.

5. *Distributors* are individuals or organizations who take your products, services, and/or solutions, add some kind of direct or indirect value, and resell them.

Stop reading and take a moment to list the "who's who" of your own selling process. What are your different categories of potential business relationships? Who are the most important members of each category? Write the answers on a separate sheet of paper.

MEASURE SALES PROCESS TIME

How long it takes to sell whatever it is you're selling is critical. If you want to understand how to make your sales process deliver sales and commission checks that are larger in shorter amounts of time, you'll have to concern yourself with a performance characteristic called "sales process time."

> Your biggest return on investment will come from your business partners. Find them, sell them, and nurture your business relationships with them.

> Compress your sales process! Saved time will transmit to a faster time to revenue for your organization—and greater personal revenue for you.

Sales process time is the total elapsed time it takes to move an individual or organization from the category of "suspect" to the category of "customer" (or business partner). If you've sold to more than ten customers or so, you have the history that sales process time is created from. (If not, check with other salespeople in your organization or industry to get an idea of their history.)

Once you've determined this elapsed time, you'll have to subdivide it into some number of steps that will give you visibility into how the sale was made. Here's an example of my sales process time and the steps that constitute it.

1. Send the very important top officer (CEO, president, and/or owner) a book/letter/package outlining my value proposition or send an e-presentation via the World Wide Web outlining my value proposition.
2. Call to follow up. No connection? Leave a series of voice mail messages (one each week for seven weeks or until I receive a call back).
3. Represent my value proposition via live telephone call/conference with key players or via e-presentation/video/audio, or supply other collateral as requested.
4. Sign agreement.
5. Conduct event.
6. Track and broadcast results to all other divisions/sister companies and referrals.

The first five steps of this six-step sales process take anywhere from one to four months; the average is a little over two and a half months.

• • •

Stop reading now and take a moment to quantify your own sales process time and the individual steps needed to turn a "suspect" into a "customer," "business partner," or "distributor."

Record your results now on a separate sheet of paper.

ANALYZE THE PROCESS

CEOs who sell have a keen sense of what's needed and what's excess baggage. After reviewing hundreds of sales processes, I can tell you that the quickest way to find out if they are effective and efficient is to see what steps salespeople consistently ignore. If the same three steps are being skipped over again and again by a given sales team, rest assured they're not needed.

> Follow the lead of CEOs who sell: Look for the largest sales opportunities in your territory.

Take a moment now and look in-depth at each and every step you currently are being asked to take in the process of moving a suspect to a customer/business partner/distributor. Are there any unnecessary elements of the process you're now being asked to perform for the sake of habit or internal show? Are there any elements that duplicate work someone else does (or should be doing)?

Record your analysis on a separate sheet of paper.

Here are two examples of what you might come up with:

1. *Remove.* "Get a copy of each suspect's most recent annual report." (When you come right down to it, the most important numbers and words in an annual report can be obtained from the "horse's mouth" while you're building effective business rapport.)

2. *Reposition.* "Understand the needs of each level of buying influence." (This somewhat generic request appeared in every single sales process I obtained during the research for this book. In reality, that all-encompassing request for information can and should be distilled down to a few intelligent questions sprinkled throughout the entire sales process.)

For the next ten suspects that you pursue, use your *modified* plan (with the appropriate steps eliminated or repositioned) and see if the new approach improves the:

- elapsed time to obtain the first sale.
- ease of obtaining the first sale.
- number of steps you had to take to get the first sale.
- number of steps the suspect had to take to get the first sale.
- size of the first sale.
- emotional "weather" you and the suspect encountered during the process of making the sale.

IMPROVE THE PROCESS

Like effective CEOs, we each have a responsibility to be on a constant "improvement patrol." We have to look for ideas to make whatever we use in our sales efforts work better. Improvements can affect our product/service/solution, our sales tools, and yes, ourselves and our sales process.

On a separate sheet of paper, list the first three ideas that come to mind that you and your organization could take to *immediately* improve your current sales process. Do not proceed with the rest of this chapter until you have come up with at least three ideas for improving the process.

Experiment a little. Be willing to try something for its own sake. If it works, great; if not, try something else.

CONTROL THE PROCESS

Effective CEOs are control fanatics; you should be, too.

> CEOs who sell find a repeatable sales process that works—and then stick to it.

Don't try to maintain control by breathing fire and creating fear in the office. (A side note: You'd probably be surprised at how many CEOs don't like using those tactics.) Do make sure each step of the sales process is unfolding in a timely fashion. Ultimately, that's *your* responsibility, not anyone else's.

Remember: The essence of any process is that it is predictable and yields a certain result when followed. When any step of a process is forgotten or not done on time, per plan, *the result changes.* Establish the right plan, then *follow it.* By doing so, you maintain control.

CEOs see the world as consisting of elements *they can control and repeat.* Is that a "correct" way of looking at the world? That doesn't really matter. It's a *useful* way of looking at the world. Whenever a potential sale disappoints you (the size of the sale was too small, the sale took too long, or, in the worst case, the sale didn't happen at all), you will, if you are selling like a successful CEO, ask yourself questions like, "What, if anything, did the plan overlook?" and "What did we overlook in the plan?" You will *not* ask yourself questions like, "Why do these things always happen to me?" or "Is the economy affecting our ability to sell?"

Take a moment and write down, on a separate sheet of paper, the *reason* for the last sales "disaster" you had or witnessed as a salesperson. Sorry, "The competition beat us," is not an acceptable reason. What we're looking for here is what essential step in the process was skipped, changed, or not incorporated in the first place.

REPLICATE THE PROCESS

This is the culmination of everything you've been learning about in this chapter: how to keep working the process so that you get the results you want, when you want them.

Take a look at the funnel diagram on the next page. This simple and effective visual representation is the best tool I've come across for managing and replicating the sales process. The idea is simple: Put a constant flow (not too much or too little) of suspects into the top, and you get a constant flow (just the right amount) of customers/business partners/distributors at the bottom.

> Reporting and tracking your sales process doesn't require fancy software or customized reports. Straightforward, simple summaries adorn the walls of many a CEO's office.

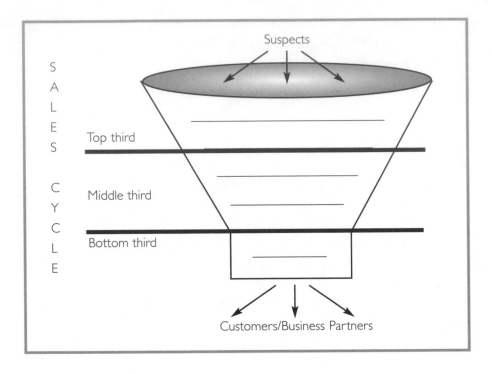

What does your funnel have to look like *now* to deliver the outcome you want *later?*

Spend 75 percent of your working time managing the 1-2-3-step process of this funnel (see below) and you'll find yourself at 125 percent of your sales quota.

Take a look at the three steps.

1. First, work the **bottom third** of your process. Bring to signature the suspects that are in this area of your funnel.

2. Next, work the **top third** of your funnel. Qualify against the right criteria; place new suspects into your process.

3. Finally, move the suspects that populate the **middle ground** into the last phases of your cycle.

Secrets of VITO

THINK

CEOs know how important it is to have a process identified for each and every critical operation in their organization—including sales. The following six-step process can be used to compare your sales process with what we know is important to a CEO.

1. *Identify the human elements of your organization's sales process.* CEOs care about the total potential of the marketplace. They measure the amount of time and resources they'll put into a relationship by the amount of potential revenue it can deliver. The key categories are: Suspects, Prospects, Customers, Business Partners, and Distributors.

2. *Measure sales process time.* CEOs know that time equals money. Sales process time is how long it takes you to sell whatever it is you're selling. It is important that you understand this number. Ask yourself, "How can I make my sales process deliver sales and commission checks that are larger—in shorter amounts of time?"

3. *Analyze the process.* CEOs know how to distinguish between what's needed and what's excess baggage. The quickest way to find out if you're operating at peak efficiency is to see what steps you're consistently ignoring in your sales process.

4. *Improve the process.* CEOs are always on the lookout for ways to improve the sales process. You should be, too.

5. *Control the process.* CEOs are control fanatics. The essence of any process is that it is predictable and yields a certain result when followed. When any step of a process is forgotten or not done on time, per plan, the result changes. So think like a CEO by establishing the right plan and then following it consistently. By doing so, you will maintain control.

6. *Replicate the process.* This is the culmination of all the previous steps. Once you get the desired result, you must keep repeating the process.

SELL

Work your sales process so you are constantly prospecting for new business, qualifying existing prospects, and opening up business relationships. The proper sequence of activity will yield greater returns for your time invested. Make sure you perform the following activities on a regular basis.

> Work on opportunities that have been in your process the longest.

> Prospect for new business (bring qualified prospects into your forecast).

> Move each prospect a step closer to becoming a customer (perform the next step: proposals, demonstrations, customer visits, etc.).

TAKE ACTION

Take your sales process and represent it in the form of a sales funnel (see page 156). This visual aid will make it extremely easy for you to see what prospects are in need of a next-step action.

> Review pages 150 and 151 and determine "who's who" in your sales process.

> Go to page 156 and complete your sales funnel.

For additional information and worksheets, visit:
www.CEOsellingtips.com
Click on: "Get Info"
Locate and download Chapter 11.

12

"Procrastination is the thief of time."

—ANONYMOUS

HOW CEOS
MANAGE TIME

S everal years ago, while on a nine-hour flight aboard a 747, I struck up a conversation with one of the flight attendants. He must have realized I was bored to tears; he asked if I would like to take a peek into the cockpit. I agreed instantly.

As we entered the dimly lit cockpit filled with hundreds of gauges, dials, buttons, and switches, I was immediately fascinated. As I sat there, I watched the pilot and copilot nonchalantly scanning the gauges, making an occasional adjustment and entering information into their onboard computers while at the same time chatting "shop talk." It was after about five minutes that I noticed

> If you're spending more than 30 percent of your work day on nonselling activities, you're not delegating effectively.

one particular dial seemed a little unusual. It looked similar to a compass but had a red light under it. Every second or so, that red light would flash several times. Neither the pilot nor the copilot seemed to notice the light flashing on and off, on and off. I wondered: Was the light of any importance? Had I discovered an emergency? Do these people know about the "red light" situation we've run into here?

After several minutes of small talk, I couldn't contain myself any longer. "Hey captain," I asked as casually as I could. "What's that red light that keeps flashing?" He looked at me and smiled. "Oh, that's the automatic pilot. It flashes every time we stray off course."

"So," I asked, "we're headed for Barbados rather than Newark, New Jersey?"

He chuckled and then explained everything to me. It turns out that during a normal flight, a Boeing 747 SP400 spends 99 percent of its time heading in the wrong direction. The vast majority of flights are successful, though, not because the autopilot is never wrong but because the corrections take place very, very quickly. The captain went on to explain that the two most important pieces of information the computer receives are—you guessed it—*where the plane is* and *where the pilot wants it to go*.

As I returned to my seat, I thought about the interesting parallel between this jumbo jet's autopilot and my own ability to manage my time.

- Both the 747 and I travel at high speeds (well, most of the time, anyway).
- We both have a known starting point and a desired ending point.
- We both are responsible for getting other individuals to their destination of choice (the jet has paying passengers; I have paying customers).
- We both are responsible for working as effectively as possible.

- We both are expected to generate revenue.

What, I asked myself, was my course-correction system?

Time Management Defined

Just about every time-management course, system, or book ever created focuses on the "management" or "control" of one's time. What seems to be ignored is the question of how one uses or consumes time.

As I interviewed CEOs for this book, I noticed their time is well protected and managed by their personal assistants, but I also noticed *they themselves* made a habit of using available time well and efficiently. Put bluntly, they course-corrected a great deal.

You'll recall the jumbo jet's autopilot needed to know exactly where its starting or takeoff point was and where it was expected to land. You're no different. You need to know exactly where you are starting and where you want to wind up at the end of each time period you want to manage and consume. All this depends on your daily, weekly, monthly, quarterly, and yearly goals.

CEOs know exactly what their short- and long-term goals are, and so should you.

LONG-TERM COURSE CORRECTION

The most popular definition of long-term goals with CEOs and the organizations they drive are goals set 12 months out. Each and every CEO I interviewed had a firm grasp and understanding of where they were starting for the year and where they wanted to end up at the end of the year. Do you?

Most salespeople know what their yearly sales quota is. Far fewer know precisely how many prospecting calls they'll need to make to *exceed* that quota. I strongly suggest that you take the time to work the following short-term quota goal exercise. It's an eye-opener.

If you contacted 100 suspects (via mail, e-mail, e-presentations, telephone calls, in-person meetings, or any combination of these), how many potential prospects would result?

Write your answer here:

(A) _____

How many of these potential prospects would turn into hot leads that have more than a 75 percent chance of becoming a customer?

Write your answer here:

(B) _____

How many of these 75 percent probabilities would turn into actual customers?

Write your answer here:

(C) _____

Now, divide the number on line (C) by 100.

Write your answer here:

(D) _____

> When you agree to do something, do it with full attention and commitment. Saving time doesn't mean taking shortcuts.

The fraction or percentage you came up with in (D) should make clear the number of sales you can expect from every 100 approaches you make on suspects.

Fill in the Blanks

What is your yearly sales quota, in dollars?

(I): $_____

If you have existing customers, and if sales to those customers count against your sales quota, write that number here:

(II): $_____

Subtract item (II) from item (I) to yield the amount of new sales dollars needed this year. Write that number here:

(III): $_____

Enter the dollar amount of your average new sale: (IV): $_____

Divide item (III) by item (IV) to yield the number of new sales needed this year. Then divide by (D).

(V): _____/_____

If you're going to hit any target in business, you must clearly identify that target. Make sure you complete the simple exercise shown above, and don't wait too long to audit your calculations. Over the next 30 days, monitor and validate your base numbers (A, B, C, and D). If they're not accurate, you won't be standing in the winner's circle at the end of the year.

> Multiply your efforts! Whenever you visit a prospect or customer, make sure you call on someone new in the organization.

SHORT-TERM COURSE CORRECTION

The most popular definition of short-term goals with CEOs and the organizations they drive are goals set for each quarter. If you completed the exercise above, you quickly calculated your long- and short-term goals for your sales quota. But numbers are just a part of the entire picture.

CEOs Know How to Micromanage Their Time, and So Should You

For the next two weeks, keep track of where you're spending your time and what you're doing. At the end of the two weeks, take a highlighter and mark all the activities you engaged in that were not directly related to overachieving your goals.

Learn to steal time from the activities that do not directly support your goals. Learn to put tasks together to save time. Here's an example: If you're going to take a prospect to lunch, always invite a customer along. If you can't get a customer to join you, take your customer support, marketing, or engineering manager. It's a perk for your team member and a good demonstration of your organization's talent.

CEOs Know How to Say "No" Without Ever Saying It, and So Should You

The word "no" (phrased properly, of course) is a simple and powerful time-saving device.

Customer: *John, can you stop by tomorrow morning and take a look at the quality of the copies the 1244 you sold us is making?*

Salesperson who is a poor time manager: *Sure, I'll change my morning around and get there by 11 o'clock.*

Salesperson who is a good time manager/user: *The quality of your documents is important to me, but I'm afraid I have appointments scheduled for the entire day. Let me get our service department on the line, and they'll send a technician out first thing in the morning. I'll plan on calling you tomorrow afternoon to make sure everything is OK with the 1244. Before I connect you to them, is there anything else I can get for you?*

Know when to say "no." Whenever anything (except an emergency or a request from your own top officer) threatens to take time away from your core activities that directly support your short- and/or long-term goals, *just say no*—politely. It will feel selfish at first, but in time you'll get used to it, and the people who request your "immediate attention" will catch on, too.

CEOs Take Time to Fill Their Cup, and So Should You

I've yet to meet a successful CEO who didn't take the time to have a vacation. They trust people on their team as much as they trust themselves to carry the torch and keep the ball rolling.

You can only give as much as you have. If your energy is low and you're all stressed out, you won't be able to give your job your best effort. Never stop the process; empower your team to carry it forward, and occasionally take time out to recharge your attitude.

Never, ever let your vacation time carry forward into the next year. Use it *this* year.

CEOs Spend More Time Being Proactive than Reactive, and So Should You

Anticipate the needs of your prospects, customers, and team members, and you'll have plenty of time to spare. That's good advice if, at the end of the day, you feel like your day controlled you instead of the other way around. The fastest way to anticipate needs is to look at the relevant history.

Take a look at your customer base. In the space below, write five requests your customers make of you that seem to repeat themselves time and again (I've provided my own customers' requests in the right column as examples.)

1. _____
1. Instant response to requests for proposals.

2. _____
2. Prompt return (next day) on all messages.

3. _____
3. On-site inventory for seminar materials.

4. _____
4. Permission to videotape live events.

5. _____
5. Right to book all travel for trainers.

Now, if I wanted to waste a whole bunch of time, I'd wait until the last minute to respond to proposals. I would let inventory drop below minimum levels and cause all sorts of emergencies that I would have to take time out to solve. I'd neglect to put in our contracts a videotaping clause allowing recording of my

Know the
difference
between short-
term and long-
term goals.

events. But I don't waste time. So I take the opposite approach in each case.

If you know that your customers have certain demands, you can count on your prospects having similar ones. Be prepared to answer, handle, respond to, and resolve issues *before* they arise, and you'll save untold hours and effort.

MORE ON SHORT-TERM GOALS

Here is a shortlist of other important goals that CEOs embrace. Make a check mark alongside the ones you currently have on your list of short-term goals.

1. Business soft skills development (seminars/workshops/reading)
2. Team building (writing thank-you notes, buying small gifts of appreciation)
3. Customer touch points (making phone calls, in-person visits, sending thank-you cards)
4. Industry hard skills development (reading periodicals, trade publications)
5. Competitive knowledge (identification and understanding of competitors)
6. Community outreach (philanthropic endeavors)
7. Marketplace outreach (presentations at various organizations to raise brand awareness)
8. Direct support of the sales process
9. Direct support of the marketing process
10. Direct support of the engineering process
11. Direct support of the manufacturing process
12. Direct support of the financial process

The first eight are easy to understand and map over to your short-term goals, but you may have a few questions about numbers nine through twelve.

If you want to sell like a CEO, you'll need to have a working understanding of your company's marketing, engineering, manufacturing, and financial processes. Why? Imagine you're in a meeting with a top officer in a prospective account. The CEO asks you your marketing and manufacturing operations methods to keep inventory on the shelves so shipments are made in a timely fashion. Don't you want to have the answer?

Secrets of VITO

THINK

CEOs know it, and so do you: Time well spent on the right tasks spells success. It doesn't matter what time management system you use, the principles that follow are the cornerstones of good, sound time management for your sales process.

SELL

> Know how to micromanage your time. Simply stated, spend the majority of your time on tasks that directly support the over-achievement of your goals.
> Know how and when to use the word "no" (phrased properly, of course).
> Take time to fill your cup. Salespeople who don't take vacations because they're too busy are missing the point. You can't manage your time or anything else if you're burned-out.
> Spend more time being proactive than reactive. Reacting wastes time.

Know the difference between short- and long-term goals. How many sales calls must you make to find a qualified prospect? How many qualified prospects does it take before you find a customer, business partner, or distributor?

TAKE ACTION

Ponder the list of five repetitive requests customers make of you on page 165 and compile your own list of time-savers.

For additional information and worksheets, visit:
www.CEOsellingtips.com
Click on: "Get Info"
Locate and download Chapter 12.

PART 5

CEOs Guide You

13

---

*"Failure is only the opportunity to begin again
more intelligently."*

—HENRY FORD

CEOs
DEFINE SUCCESS

W e've reached the point where you'll be getting your lessons straight from the top.

We'll start with what could be the biggest lesson—what success is and how it comes about. We'll begin our exploration by
looking at Howard Putnam, past CEO of Southwest Airlines,
which is, as these words are being written, the only U.S.-owned
and U.S.-operated airline actually making a profit. That fact, I
believe, is strong testimony to the quality of the vision, mission,
and ideas that Putnam helped to create and make part of the
day-to-day culture at Southwest.

Let's hear what this visionary leader has to say about what
goes into *success*—into truly thinking and selling like a CEO.

VISION

Any organization or individual hoping to thrive in today's unpredictable economic environment would do well to maintain a clear vision of *why* it makes sense to show up for work every day. I'm talking about an easy-to-understand mission statement that answers the question, What are we all about?

Of all the individuals I interviewed for this book, Howard Putnam stands out as the ultimate "champion of vision."

After his successful run at Southwest, he took over as CEO at ailing Braniff Airlines. There he was faced with running an operation that was hemorrhaging money. Putnam had to right-size the company, re-engineer and revitalize the public's image of the airline, and put the firm back in the black—and he had to do it quickly. He called upon his clear, laser-beam focus for rallying employees. He recalls asking all 10,000 employees for three ideas apiece on how they would turn around and save the airline. No idea was a bad idea; he wanted it all. He received more than 3,000 responses. Putnam sent a handwritten note to each and every person who had mustered up an idea. Years later, he met one of the 3,000 recipients of his personal touch. He was amazed to learn that the person still had the note.

Putnam's stiff setbacks at Braniff never shook his personal sense of why he was doing what he was doing. He communicated that feeling of confidence and directed it to everyone at Braniff. People came to sense that he was committed to acting in their best interests... and that he did this not as an abstract ideal but as part of his own deepest identity.

How important is having a crystal-clear vision of exactly what the company's mission is? Let's ask Putnam.

Vision is critically important when it comes to training your customers on what your mission statement really means. It's critically important when it comes to showing your marketplace (investors, for instance) your team members. And it's a critically important part of the process of making sure all your team members become salespeople.

Do you have a clear understanding of your vision? Or is it just an ideal? Have you recruited *your* team to help you "brainstorm" your mission? Is your mission clear to your prospects and customers? (Do they even know it?) Have you clearly defined success? (If not, how will you know when you've achieved it?)

If you're going to think and sell like a successful CEO, it's imperative that everyone around you knows where you're going, how long it will take you to get there, and what you'll do upon your arrival. You must transform your ideals—that is, your principles, standards, morals, and ethics—into a vision, and take action on that vision to create success for everyone with whom you do business.

> The first rule in the CEO's sales book is that *everyone* is a salesperson, and it's *everyone's* job to sell *every day!*

Of course, in this process you, like Putnam, are more likely than not to run into experiences that some would use the "F" word (failure) to define. How *you* define those experiences—how you incorporate them into your vision—is what will make all the difference.

Successful CEOs like Putnam know that our best lessons come from mistakes. They know that "failing" at *something* is a far better outcome than "succeeding" at *nothing* through lack of action.

We do not "fail" until we turn a learning experience into a negative judgment against ourselves, our vision, our mission, or our team. In fact, if you put six simple words in front of each statement that follows, you'll be taking the first step to put failure in its proper perspective. The six words are:

I didn't fail, I suffered from...

1. *lack of focus or purpose*—that ability to keep our "eyes on the road."
2. *incomplete or incorrect information*—an insistence on moving ahead even if we don't have enough facts.
3. *lack of drive*—the pattern of giving up too early or not recognizing more creative options.

Putnam's indomitable spirit impressed me profoundly. He is truly the kind of person who never, ever fails.

OTHER THOUGHTS ON SUCCESS FROM CEOs WHO SELL

Here are some other core observations on the ingredients of success; each is from a CEO who takes pride in his or her ability to sell.

Knowledge and Experience

Joe Gustafson learned the importance of laserlike focus, correct information, and continual drive early on in the process of building his internet-based presentation company, Brainshark. Here's what he had to say about how knowledge and experience support success.

> Let fear inspire, not paralyze you for your next challenge.

My strongest sales trait is putting my past failures and successes and the insights I've learned to work on the problem at hand. Knowledge of my business and the industry help me to be "cautiously driven"—so I don't fall on my sword.

Gustafson also knows (and happily volunteers) his most profound *weakness* in any sales situation—a weakness that many CEOs share. Can you guess what it is? It's a deal killer, something I call "sales prevention." It's misused and/or misguided ego.

Be Authentic and Take Control

Karin Bellintoni, CEO of I-Mark, has mastered the art of getting noticed. She took this art to new heights when she masterminded a way for her clients to double the response rate of the typical direct-mail campaign while at the same time cutting in half the cost of capture.

In Bellintoni's words:

> *I know what it takes to get people to call me back: I give people an immediate sense of me. I am authentic, and I take control right away! Be yourself.... The only business you're really in is the people business.*

Serve the Best Interests of Others

Look how similarly focused the following definitions are. These are the answers I got when I asked top CEOs to tell me what success meant to them.

> *Helping people that want to win... win.*
> —Jay Rodgers, Chairman of the Board, Smart Start Inc.

> *Helping others first... then helping myself.*
> —Joe Mancuso, President, CEO Club

> *Giving something of lasting value.*
> —John Brown, Tri-Steel Corp.

> *Helping others get to the top of their mountain.*
> —Robert Posten, Landis Strategy & Innovation

> *Leaving a bigger footprint in the sand than my shoe size.*
> —Dock Houk, CEO, National Heritage Foundation

There's a lesson to be drawn from these remarkably similar definitions. It sounds simple but is actually quite profound.

Serve the best interests of others.

They, in turn, will serve you.

If your definition of success doesn't include helping someone else to make the most of life—**change it**! A definition of success that focuses solely on monetary rewards will not serve you in the long run (and probably not in the short run, either).

In the final analysis, success really isn't about winning at the expense of others. It's more about a *multilateral* win. Perhaps the CEO who best exemplifies this win-win approach is Jay Rodgers, Chairman of the Board of Smart Start Inc. He learned to redefine the meaning of a winning partnership from his father. In fact, Rodgers actually created a company around his father's belief about a 50/50 deal. It's called 70/70 Incorporated, and it follows Rodger's Senior's 70/70 rule.

> End-of-month or end-of-quarter gimmicks won't help you be perceived as someone who adds value.

The 70/70 rule goes like this: Each person or partner in a relationship must be committed to do 70 percent of the work. In other words, without worrying what the other partner is doing, each person in the 50/50 relationship must commit independently to *70* percent of the work and put forth 70 percent of the effort. Imagine the outcome if each and every partner did that. Instead of maxing out at a feeble 100 percent, the partnership would enjoy a robust 140 percent achievement level.

Be Courageous

The dictionary defines "courage" as the ability to face danger, difficulty, threats, or physical pain without fear. Actually, I think anyone who faces danger, difficulty, threats, or physical pain without fear is not courageous but stupid. Everyone feels fear;

the trick is to understand it, to control it, to put it in its place, and to learn from it when appropriate. If you try to eradicate fear entirely, you'll end up either psychotic or disappointed or both.

A more realistic definition of the word "courageous," and one I prefer, is that of Jennifer Ash, CEO of Tomco Tool & Die, who emphasizes the kind of courage that is based on *identifying and trusting one's instincts*. Ash operates a successful organization in the tool and die industry, an industry that, for all intents and purposes, is totally dominated by men. Ash is the heir to her father's patented process and his successful business. You can imagine how much courage Ash has to muster when eroding market share, encroaching offshore competition, and top-down reorganizations are a necessary part of her day-to-day operations.

I asked Ash what she looks for in a business ally. Here's what she had to say:

> Top CEOs tap into their intuition on a daily basis. Do you?

> *First and foremost, I trust my intuition—and only then make an overall assessment. I look at the total person, not just one aspect of their personality or behavior. I am cautioned by someone who tries too hard.*

Ash possesses real courage—the kind of courage that's rooted in awareness and understanding, open evaluation of the circumstances, and trust in one's own intuitive responses. This type of courage makes success a reality.

Be Persistent—and Never Stop Learning

Persistence simply means coming back, again and again, to the tasks of attaining one's goal. There is a big difference between being persistent and being a pest. The persistent person tries all possible angles and thinks up a few new ones for good measure in working to overcome objections, obstacles, and doubt. By contrast, pests rarely bring anything new to the situation. They simply make the same calls, ask the same questions, and apply the same annoying strategies without ever monitoring what's working and what isn't.

Persistent people inspire unshakable confidence; they seem to have an internal equanimity, a peace of mind that lets others know everything's going to be all right. Pests act as though the world were about to end. They're big on crises—and they make a habit of putting their "stuff" on everyone around them.

As a lesson in persistence, consider the words of Joe Mancuso, who is the founder and CEO of the CEO Club. Mancuso has met more CEOs than anyone else in the world. He has 40,000 CEOs on his mailing list. It's the largest organization of its kind in the world. I asked Mancuso to share the most critical lesson he has learned from his peers. Here's his answer:

> CEOs don't fail. Their efforts do.

Failure is a resting place. Somewhere you catch your breath. All you have to do is pick yourself up one more time than your nearest competitor.

Mancuso knows that persistence applies, first and foremost, to the expansion of the human mind. When I asked him about his plan for self-improvement, he told me he tries to learn from his peers. How, I asked, does he do that? Here's what I heard in response:

> *I ask two questions of each CEO that I meet. These questions tell me a lot about the person and their leadership style, and they also tell me whether I can learn from this person. I ask, "Describe your most significant accomplishment," and "Describe your most significant failure." Then I shut up and listen.*

This kind of persistence is deeply allied with loyalty; it inspires people, expands the knowledge base, and builds up relationships. It instills trust and always puts the other person's best interests first.

Secrets of VITO

THINK

Thinking clearly and staying focused on your goals is a lot easier said than done. Competitive pressures, economic downturns, budget cutbacks, and product delays are just some of the situations that may contribute to a loss of focus on your objectives. Here are five "CEO-think" strategies for keeping your eyes on the prize when times get tough.

1. *Write an easy-to-understand mission statement* that answers the question, "What are we all about?" Every successful CEO has a statement like this, and so should you.

2. *Constantly ask yourself,* "What can I learn from this situation that will help me move forward on my goals?" The key is not to let your ego get in the way of learning. CEOs learn from every interpersonal situation, no matter what the other person's uniform happens to be, and so should you.

3. *Stay flexible.* Forget about attaining perfection; move past setbacks, try new approaches, and look for new and more effective ways to achieve the desired results.

4. *Move past fear.* During tough times, successful CEOs push past the rest of the crowd. Everyone feels fear; the trick is to control it, to put it in its place, and to learn from it when appropriate.

5. *Be persistent.* Every CEO I interviewed for this book developed the knack for coming back, again and again, to the tasks necessary to attain their goals. They didn't stop after hitting what others may interpret as an impossible-to-overcome obstacle.

SELL

Take the five success traits that you just read about and put them to use in your next new sales opportunity by asking yourself:

➤ What's my purpose/mission in this sale?

➤ What past experience can I call upon to help me make this sale?

➤ What can I do or say that will show my strongest authentic sales trait to this prospect?

➤ What can I do, say, or show this prospect that would set me and my product, service, or solution apart from the rest?

➤ How will I communicate with my new prospect so I can persist in making this sale without appearing to be a pest?

TAKE ACTION

Pick at least one role model who exemplifies the five success elements you just read. Then *learn all you possibly can about that person*, whether he or she is a local business leader, a colleague at work, or even a historical figure.

Before you finalize your choice, consider this: Successful people are internally secure enough to experiment time and time again. They are *unstoppable*. They've got that "no matter what" attitude that we all had when we were toddlers first learning to walk. I've known more than one successful CEO who could be described as "childlike" in this respect. Make sure your role model displays this critical "immature" trait.

14

"The highest regard for a person's toil is not what
they get for it, but what they become by it."

—JOHN RUSKIN

THE SALES
LEADERSHIP MISSION

H ow do CEOs who sell build a sense of mission with their
prospects, customers, and key team members? You'll find
out in this chapter, which shows us how two of today's most
dynamic corporate leaders use *personal beliefs* to support their
sales processes.

BELIEVING IN YOURSELF, YOUR COMPANY,
AND WHAT YOU SELL

Jim Amos, former CEO of Mail Boxes Etc., is big on believing
not only in his abilities but also in the value his company delivers and the abilities of his team.

Here's some of what Jim had to share about passion and
belief:

Knowledge-based workers own the knowledge we don't. They may obtain information from our systems, but they individually own the knowledge. People run the systems—the systems don't run the people. Knowledge-based workers must be passionate about their purpose, beliefs, and mission; they must have and then apply their discretionary energy with all of that in mind.

My job is simply to keep the dream in front of them—to keep the Mail Boxes Etc. dream in the forefront of their minds at all times.

But it doesn't stop there. The sales process is about constant communication. My job is to be popular and "well known"— someone who constantly shares the dream with customers, with board members, with employees, and with franchise owners.

Basically, I believe that courage is a work ethic. That means that I must respect my people and allow them to retain their own dignity. I lead not with an anvil but with benchmarks.

> CEOs who sell know that trust and core values are what make successful business relationships possible.

Sharing the dream (or, if you prefer, the vision), is, of course, just as important when interacting with your own sales team members as it is when you're meeting with a CEO from another organization. To share the dream, you must, as Amos notes, embody it wherever you go and broadcast it to every "customer" you meet, whether that customer is internal or external. Amos is a great role model for that kind of passionate commitment to his company's dream—its mission.

Amos also told me:

My conviction is that unshakable trust, solid core personal values, integrity, and honesty pave the way to a successful relationship in all business and personal endeavors.

I can personally attest that Amos lives up to that high standard. I can also attest that he tries not to let anything build unnecessary obstacles between himself and those he connects with. "When I make a mistake," Amos told me, "I show the humor of it; I laugh at myself and allow others to laugh at me, too. And then I move on. Relationships are built in the trenches; that's where the real tests come.... Being truthful in how you react to a situation: That's what matters most."

THE POWER OF PURPOSEFUL BELIEF

To learn how to put the power of purposeful belief to work in accomplishing your own mission, you'll need to do what Jim has done and continues to do on a daily basis. You'll need to get in touch with what gives you that power in the first place: you.

> Understand your own current opinions, beliefs, and convictions—and rebuild them as necessary to support the life you want to adopt.

In the end, *you* are your own best ally—or your most formidable competitor—when it comes to harnessing a sense of mission and purpose. This intangible, indefinable quality, essential to successful interactions with top "C-level" decision-makers and approvers, either strengthens your own opinions, beliefs, and convictions... or doesn't.

Take a quick look now at what Amos emphasized when I asked him about the mission of sales leadership: opinions, beliefs, and convictions. (Note: I'm basing what follows on my discussions with Amos and also on my knowledge of how CEOs tend to operate.)

- *Opinions* fall short of having the need for positive knowledge. An opinion is a combination of facts and ideas that can be true, or are likely to be proven true, but that may not be. (Many opinions, of course, share a fuzzy border with those disempowering "D"s, delusion and denial.) It is possible to have one or more opinions on the same topic.

It's also acceptable in the business world of a CEO to change an opinion when it becomes necessary (or politically wise) to do so. There are occasions when CEOs have no opinion whatsoever on an important business topic, but they're quite rare.

- *Beliefs* are based on specific past experiences, generalizations, or conjecture. Once a belief is obtained, it's generally held to be true and is rarely challenged or changed. Sometimes we are tempted to defend our beliefs to the bitter end, even when there may be no factual basis for the belief.

- *Convictions* are certainties of the mind in either of the two previous categories—that is, fully settled opinions or assured beliefs. Once established, convictions defy alteration. In extreme situations, convictions can cause serious financial, social, and/or physical setbacks. On the other hand, convictions can also be responsible for total success in every aspect of business and life.

THE CONSTRUCTIVE BELIEF SYSTEMS OF CEOs

During my interview with Peter Bell, the co-founder and CEO of StorageNetworks, he shared with me his strong belief about his involvement in the sales process.

> *I believe strongly that I must routinely "disrupt" the sales process—from the standpoint of shortening the sales cycle— by doing a "title-to-title" call or in-person meeting. In all of these cases, though, I will still hold my sales team responsible for working the sales process.*

Bell believes that involving himself in the sales process has a clear benefit: shortening the amount of time it takes to turn a suspect into a customer. He has amassed so much evidence for this belief, in fact, that it has taken on the form of a conviction.

Could Bell's belief be changed? Perhaps, but I doubt it. Why? Because the emphasis he put on the word "strongly" gave me the sense that he had invested himself in this way of looking at the world and that employing this vantage point had paid off for him handsomely. Bell has developed a *constructive belief system* about involving himself in the sales process.

Does that belief, that sense of conviction in what his company has to offer pay off? Consider the following story Bell told me:

> *For two hours, a C-level prospect spoke of nothing but what our competition could do for his company.* [But nonetheless, Peter stayed his course and made his presentation.] *I thanked him for his time and hospitality. I gave the deal a 50/50 chance. Two days later, he called me and gave us the business.*

TAKE CONTROL OF YOUR OWN
BELIEFS AND CONVICTIONS

It's virtually impossible to understate the importance of beliefs when it comes to harnessing the power of a CEO who sells. Once you take total responsibility for your own empowering beliefs and convictions, you will, by definition, be thinking, acting, and selling like a successful CEO.

> Have a sense of conviction in what you and your company offer.

Perhaps it's time to examine some of your own beliefs. Here are some examples of what I call self-limiting, "killer beliefs":

- CEOs would never take time out of their busy day to see me. (After having met with hundreds of CEOs, I can attest that this one doesn't withstand the test of experience.)
- I have nothing to offer this person.
- I'll never make "salesperson of the year"—my territory isn't good enough.
- CEOs make me nervous.

- I choke under pressure.
- CEOs are difficult people to talk with.
- My parents ruined me for life. (I think we should all get rid of that one!)

- _____

- _____

I left some room to add a few just in case I missed one or two of your favorites; add your own "killer beliefs" above before proceeding.

Each of the negative beliefs has a corresponding *positive* counterpart. (For instance, "I can add significant value to the day of the highest-positioned person in any organization.") Take a moment now to write *positive, empowering beliefs* on a separate sheet of paper; make sure to compose one for each negative belief you feel you may now be harboring.

CHANGE YOUR OWN BELIEFS
AND SELL LIKE A CEO ON A MISSION

Use new information, emotion, and social proof to change your own belief system.

It's not always easy, but beliefs can be changed. It's a matter of applying the right stimuli and taking advice from the top. Let's start by focusing on the three conditions necessary for our minds to change or adopt a new belief or strengthen an existing one. When we're done, we'll take a look at a list of core empowering beliefs that the most effective CEOs have—the beliefs that make their sales meetings less like presentations and more like divinely ordained missions.

What have you got to do to change a belief?

- *Gather or create new information.* The more supportive information you add, the stronger your belief will become, until it eventually develops into a conviction.

Because convictions tend to stick around forever, the ones we embrace have a huge impact on the quality of our lives and the success of our business endeavors. The right convictions can mean prosperity, optimism, and happiness. Latching on to the wrong convictions, on the other hand, can literally kill you. So focus on the right stuff. (Note: You've already taken a huge step in that direction; by reading this book, you are gathering new, positive, empowering information that will help you begin to change your beliefs about selling.)

- *Add emotion.* Once you gather your new information, you'll need to apply your emotions to the process. The greater the emotions, the greater the speed at which the new positive belief will move toward the level of a conviction—a "way of life." The greater the emotional experience we connect with a belief, the stronger the belief tends to become. (Example: At the conclusion of my interview with Jim Amos, he gave me a bear hug. Let me tell you what that did for my beliefs and convictions about this man, his mission, and his purpose. I am now ferociously proud to be one of Jim's allies, and I know I'm not the only one who feels that way about working with him.)

- *Gather social proof.* If icons of the film review industry Ebert and Roeper give a film "two thumbs up," millions of people are likely to attend that film with the expectation that they will enjoy it, which certainly doesn't hurt the odds that they actually will. This illustrates the power of social proof as a reinforcer of beliefs, positive or negative. So choose the experts you decide to "tune in to" carefully. (How's this for an example of social proof: From the moment you drive into the parking lot of Mail Boxes Etc., you can see the recognition that is paid to the company's management and top producers. Covered parking is provided for all key employees and top producers, with their names and titles proudly displayed. As soon as you enter the lobby, you can clearly see all the recognition plaques hanging on a "wall of honor." Constructive social proof is everywhere you look.)

Six Questions

The table was set for a lovely Thanksgiving dinner. Just before the honey-cured ham went into the oven, Doris cut about one inch off each side and then placed the ham squarely into the pan. Why, her husband asked, did she cut the ends off the ham?

"That's the way my mother taught me," she answered. "I've been doing it this way for years—it must have something to do with preserving the flavor."

Sure enough, the ham came out sweet and moist. After dinner, Doris's husband couldn't help asking his mother-in-law how cutting off an inch of ham on each side helped to retain flavor in the meat.

"That's the way my mother taught me," came the response. "I don't know why it makes the ham taste better, but it must do something."

There was a strange pause. Then Grandma spoke up in a soft voice.

"Oh, honey—I only cut the edge of the ham off because we never had a pot big enough to hold a good-sized ham."

Some beliefs really are worth challenging. You may learn that they don't add anything.

When you want to rid yourself of any beliefs that aren't serving you well, ask yourself the following six questions. Take 20 minutes or so to write the answers down. Be sure your answers are scrupulously honest.

1. Where did I get this belief?
2. How long ago did I adopt this belief?
3. Have I ever compromised this belief? If so, how many times? How long ago? Why?
4. What have been the consequences, if any, of compromising this belief?
5. What have been the consequences, if any, of maintaining this belief?
6. What would happen to my health, finances, and personal and professional life if I eliminated this belief?

PRINCIPLES FOR SALES LEADERSHIP

Over the past 28 years, I've worked with a good many CEOs and top-producing salespeople. I challenge you to put their principles of sales leadership to work during the next situation in your professional life that requires positive change.

> CEOs who sell emphasize accountability, confidence, curiosity, generosity, and a willingness to embrace new situations.

- *They're accountable.* They live by a code: "If it's to be, it's up to me."
- *They're confident.* They have a strong belief and faith in themselves, and they constantly reinforce that belief.
- *They want to find out more.* They're in constant search mode; they want to find ways to improve themselves, develop their strengths, and understand their weaknesses.
- *They're generous.* They're always trying to find ways to help others grow and develop.
- *They embrace new situations and actively look for new challenges.* They look at change as an opportunity to benefit by using each of the above strengths, making them even stronger and more resilient.

Secrets of VITO

THINK

CEOs are big on believing. It forms the core of their business interactions. Therefore, it makes sense that they in turn look for similar levels of belief from the individuals they choose to do business with.

Beliefs are the basis for most of our behavior, and it's impossible to mask them. If you totally believe in what you sell, that belief will come through loud and clear with no effort on your part. The opposite is also true.

SELL

What beliefs are sending the wrong message to you, your prospects, and your customers? They might sound like this: "Technology is too complex." "My territory is too small." "My prospects are not risk takers." "The competition is too stiff in this niche." "My product needs a revamping to be more competitive." "Our price really is too high." (And so on.)

If you want to change any belief you have, ask yourself the following questions:

1. *Where did I get this belief?* Was it from direct, personal experience or hearsay?

2. *How long ago did I adopt this belief?* Was it within the past year? Or during your childhood years?

3. *Have I ever compromised this belief?* If so, how many times? How long ago? Why? (Note: the more specific and accurate you can be about the "why" in this question, the better your chance will be of changing your belief.)

4. *What have been the consequences, if any, of compromising this belief?* Here again, be as specific as possible.

5. *What have been the consequences, if any, of maintaining this belief?* Does having this belief limit you in any way?

6. *What would happen to my health, finances, and personal and professional life if I eliminated this belief forever?* This is the big question.

TAKE ACTION

If you're looking for an uplifting set of beliefs, use the CEOs I interviewed for this chapter as models. Here are five pieces of advice for strengthening your core belief system. Try to become more:

> *accountable.* Live by the code: "If it's to be, it's up to me."
> *confident.* Develop a strong belief and faith in yourself, and constantly reinforce that belief.
> *curious.* Be in a constant search mode; find ways to improve yourself, develop your strengths, and understand and learn from your weaknesses.
> *generous.* Always try to find ways to help others grow and develop.
> *willing to embrace new situations.* Actively look for new challenges. Look at change as an opportunity to benefit by using each of the above strengths, making them even stronger and more resilient.

And finally, identify at least one relationship with a customer or prospect that suffered as a result of one of your negative beliefs; then use what you've learned in this chapter to modify and forever change that one "sales-limiting" belief. Make sure that you use your new empowering belief in your next sales situation.

15

"In today's economy their are no experts, no 'best and brightest' with all the answers. It's up to each one of us. The only way to screw up is to not try anything."

—THOMAS J. PETERS

CEOs'
NEW WORLD ECONOMY
SALES CAMPAIGNS

Please answer the following questions with total honesty:

- Do you feel it takes too much time for you to find a new prospect?
- Do you feel it takes you too much time to make a sale?
- Do you have doubts that the size of each initial sale is large enough to cover your cost of sales—or even that there's a wide enough margin for the sale to be profitable?
- Is add-on business from your existing customer base too low or nonexistent?
- Is your existing customer base eroding?
- Are you losing key customers to your competition?

If you answered "yes" to any of these questions, your organization may be suffering from what I call the "new world economy blues." In this chapter, we'll be discussing how CEOs who sell have found their way around these problems, which are rooted in declining attention spans, brutally increased competition, and ever-increasing depersonalization in business relationships, arising from misuse or overuse of today's communications technology and the simple fact that today, for the first time, sellers outnumber buyers.

How do CEOs who sell close *bigger* deals, *faster*, and with a greater level of *personal involvement* with the prospect than anyone else? Some of the answers are in this chapter.

> Customers vote with their feet. You'll find out too late if they walk. CEOs who sell secure existing customer loyalty by personally getting involved with key customers. You should, too.

NEW WORLD ECONOMY WEAPON 1: MARKETING MOBILITY

Kevin Dyevich, CEO of Comfort Direct, knows the importance of marketing mobility. He and his partner are the creators of a patented mattress whose manufacturing details are a closely guarded trade secret. (Believe me when I tell you this mattress provides a truly extraordinary, great night's sleep.)

Dyevich's vision is to become the world's largest manufacturer and distributor of mattresses—and he's well on his way. In the process of bringing his mattress to market, he has started a marketing revolution, a revolution that plays into the new world we are all selling in. Why? Because he uses "marketing mobility." Let's take a look at Dyevich's first major sale.

Kevin Dyevich's Story

Dyevich's first really big sale was made to a very large hotel chain. (If you've ever traveled outside your home, read a magazine, or picked up a newspaper, you have seen the name of this chain.) Dyevich's cost of sales for landing this customer was the cost of one of his mattresses plus shipping it and a few phone calls. I'll let him tell the short version of his story:

> *I sent the CEO and his wife one of our mattresses. Shortly afterwards, I got a call from one of the CEO's top staffers with a request for a meeting. The order is so big that our small manufacturing facility can't meet the demand. So—we're going to license them to build our mattress, and they're going to help us market it!*

This illustrates a key principle of selling like a CEO: Wherever possible, multiply your effects, not your efforts. Each one of your prospects must have the ability to tender more than one sale. *They* must be conduits for marketing mobility.

In Dyevich's case, his first big sale isn't the biggest sale he'll make from this transaction. Listen in, and he'll tell you why.

> Ask yourself: How else can I use this information in an ethical way to expand my customer base?

> *When each guest checks out, they'll get a pitch about the mattress, my mattress that they slept on. Can you imagine it? We hit them with the wake-up call and the check-out pitch—and a 25 percent discount coupon!*

This concept fits a dizzying array of products, services, and solutions. You get the idea: *Always pick a prospect that has depth of market and can lead you to future business.* In other words, always pick a prospect that can take you to many more prospects (I like to use a multiplier of at least ten, preferably more).

NEW WORLD ECONOMY WEAPON 2: ITTP

How do you make sure something like a marketing mobility initiative actually works? By building key values in your organization—and living up to them. Those key values, according to one

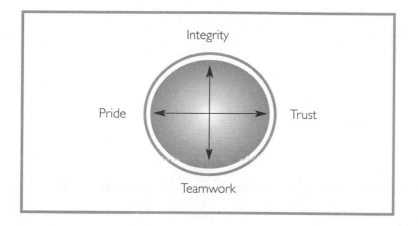

of the CEOs I interviewed, are integrity, trust, teamwork, and pride (ITTP).

Take the advice of Fred W. Green, CEO of three tremendously successful businesses. He's also on 30 boards of directors. Here's what Green has to say about this all-important topic:

> *Relationship life cycles must start during your first interaction. Approach your prospects with integrity, trust, teamwork, and pride.*

Apply Green's relationship life cycle to our marketing mobility scheme.

> Build the words "integrity," "trust," "teamwork," and "pride" into your self-talk.

Integrity

Do what you say you're going to do, and say what you're going to do. It's always been that simple for Green. Maybe it's got something to do with the teachings of Green's dad, a tough Northeast Millwright mechanic. In his honor, I'll quote Green's dad here: "Integrity is a dual-edged sword. Not only must you tell the truth, but you must also be willing to hear the truth."

Always write your request into your terms and conditions of the sale. Don't be shy about including a clause in your contract that states exactly what your customers will be doing for you. The following statement, or something pretty darn close, will work just fine:

Within 30 days of purchase and satisfaction, the client, [Beakerson Plastics], will provide to the contractor, [Jennings Materials], a list containing no fewer than ten referrals. The contractor will provide the client with all materials for pre-approval that will be sent to the list of referrals.

Now all you have to do is act with integrity. Say what you're going to do (see above). And do what you say you're going to do: Deliver the product to the satisfaction of the client.

Trust

Fred Green defines the word "trust" as "the responsibility to put no limit on success and support. Your business relationships and the partners that make them up should enable both parties to feel totally comfortable with the prospect of closing their eyes and falling backward." He mentions that he is an alumni of many Dale Carnegie courses and, in fact, aspired to become a Carnegie instructor. Green continues:

Putting the other person first is what's most important in a business relationship. When you put the other person first, you tell that person that you trust him or her. You're actually interested in seeing them do something bigger and better than anything you can do. No one has any reason to doubt the intentions of the other party.

Teamwork

Green's thinking along these lines is as follows:

Teamwork is about each member of the team ... working. If you've got a nonproducer, eliminate that person from the team.

Let's revisit Dyevich's mattress deal. Suppose that major hotel chain provided Dyevich with a coupon to include with each of the mattresses he sold. The coupon could offer a 10 percent discount on a night's lodging stating the recipient "could be sleeping like a baby away from home, too." Now that's a team that's working.

Launch, maintain, and grow business relationships that are based on finding out what's most important to the other person.

Pride

This last phase of Green's relationship life cycle really is the backbone of marketing mobility. Why? Because each partner must bring value to the table, and value is worth being proud of. It's as simple as that.

Approach your prospects with pride!

NEW WORLD ECONOMY WEAPON 3: EARLY, DIRECT, AND ACTIVE INVOLVEMENT WITH THE PRODUCT OR SERVICE

Many CEOs who sell know the value of getting prospects actively involved in the discussion/evaluation process, but there is one gentleman in particular who pushes the envelope in this area. He's Joe Sugarman, CEO of JS&A Group and creator of the legendary BluBlocker sunglasses. Joe is considered by many marketers to be the "father of infomercials."

Sugarman puts involvement at the head of the list when it comes to marketing and sales tools. He should know—his advertisements and infomercials have resulted in sales of hundreds of thousands of his patented sunglasses. This is a man who knows how to engage and involve observers. (I've seen him in action— believe me, he does.)

> CEOs who sell know that marketing and sales go hand-in-glove. Both are necessary for a successful campaign. How much do you know about your organization's marketing plan?

Whether you're selling Lear jets or laser printers, get your prospects to emotionally connect with your message, your company, and your benefits. In a face-to-face selling environment, that means personal contact with you and what you offer. People should touch your product or experience your service as soon and as often as possible. It's *always* best to be present if you can while the prospect is experiencing your product.

This principle, which we might call "the power of touch," is a big part of the success of Doug Simon's company. Simon is CEO of Mobility Elevator & Lift Co., a manufacturer and distributor of custom-made elevators. Some of the most prestigious penthouses in New York City sport Simon's elevators. Here's what he has to say about the importance of involvement as a sales tool.

> *Every opportunity we get, we invite our prospects into our showroom.... I even love to take phone call-ins. It surprises the hell out of the caller! I map their personality to their priorities; I sell them over the telephone whenever I can. I'll invite them to visit our web site.* [At last count, it has 500 pages!] *My job is basically to uncover needs, but nothing works as well as a ride.*

Simon personally trains all of his salespeople; his team has sold many big-dollar deals using Simon's involvement-based selling strategies. Getting personally involved with *prospects* turns them into *customers;* getting personally involved with key customers, as Simon and all the other CEOs interviewed will attest, turns them into critical business allies for your business.

Secrets of VITO

THINK

How do CEOs close *bigger* deals, *faster, with less expense,* and with a *greater level of personal involvement* than anyone else? One part of the answer is: They target a certain number of prospects that can lead *automatically* to future business.

If you want to multiply your presales results without multiplying your presales efforts, follow the lead of CEOs who sell and employ a marketing mobility strategy. Remember: The most successful CEOs make it clear, right up front, what they expect from the entire life cycle of the business relationship.

SELL

As you look in your territory and decide which prospects are more likely to support your marketing mobility strategy, make sure you:

> ➤ *approach your prospects with integrity.* State clearly what you're going to do and then deliver. Make it clear that you will expect your new customer to refer your products, services, and solutions to *their* customers.
> ➤ *add value.* Make sure that the other party knows that you're committed to helping him or her achieve something bigger and better than anything you can do on your own.
> ➤ *emphasize teamwork.* Teamwork is about each member of your marketing mobility team *working.* If you've got a nonproducer, find some other way to work with this person. *Give most of your time and attention to prospects who support your marketing mobility strategy.*

➤ *instill pride.* Talk up these key prospects to everyone you can.

TAKE ACTION

Take a moment now to identify at least ten potential organizations to participate in your marketing mobility program.

Here's how to do this:

Current Customers

- ➤ Sort your customer list, placing the best ones (biggest, happiest, most profitable) at the top of your list.
- ➤ Ask yourself: Can the customers of my best customers use my products, services, and solutions? Could my customers add value to their offerings by presenting my products, services, and solutions to their customers?
- ➤ Approach the CEO of your best customers with the marketing mobility idea for their own use with their other business partners.

New Prospects and In-Process Sales

- ➤ Identify which prospects serve a marketplace that could benefit by adding value to their customers with your products, services, and solutions.
- ➤ Approach the CEO with your marketing mobility idea; position it as a competitive advantage of doing business with your organization.

PART 6

CEOs Tell You

16

"For knowledge, too, is itself power."

—FRANCIS BACON

THE TEN COMMANDMENTS OF CEOS WHO SELL

I n this chapter, you'll learn the ten guiding principles of CEOs who sell. They come by way of a gentleman who has probably met more CEOs than anyone else in America, Joe Mancuso. As you may recall from an earlier chapter, Joe is the founder and CEO of the CEO Club.

I strongly suggest that you read the commandments in order and that you implement all of them in the order in which they're presented.

COMMANDMENT 1: CREATE A MASTERMIND COUNCIL

Mancuso's first principle: "Surround yourself with your counterparts and allies from

> A total of 40,000 CEOs have had input into what you're about to read.

other organizations; share ideas and solutions within this group."

As your career or business grows, your mastermind council should grow, too.

How you set this group up is, of course, up to you. If you're looking for a model for your own group, consider what the CEO Club has developed. Imagine the "brainpower" in a council comprising ten CEOs of ten organizations in different (noncompetitive) marketplaces. Now imagine that they meet on a monthly basis to listen to each other's challenges, collect information, and offer suggestions to each other. That's exactly what happens in Joe Mancuso's "Super Pack." Each CEO kicks in a hefty fee for the right to belong to this group. Why does he ask them to pay? For the same reason my parents made me buy my first car with money I earned. When you've made an investment, you're more likely to show up and participate.

My Advice

Make a list of ten of the top sales performers in your organization or the ten noncompeting organizations in your sales territory. Now organize a monthly in-person, telephone, or "chat-room" discussion. Each participant must bring no less than three sales-related ideas to the table for the topic of discussion. Each participant gets to ask one question that's got them "stymied." Try to get a look at people's questions and answers ahead of time; ideally, no two questions or answers should be the same. These sessions should be recorded, duplicated, and distributed to everyone in the group.

Oh, and don't forget to charge each participant somewhere around $25 per month, with all the proceeds going to a local charity.

Here's a possible series of topics for the first 12 months of your "sales mastermind" group.

- Prospecting for new business and networking
- Asking questions
- Listening
- Creating effective presentations
- Handling objections
- Closing techniques
- Negotiating
- Effective telephone opening statements
- Working with gatekeepers
- Leaving effective messages
- Writing prospecting letters
- Staying motivated
- Avoiding burnout

> CEOs don't sell alone, and neither should you. No matter what sales challenge you face, rest assured that someone else has faced it before. Take the time to seek some advice from respected peers and senior officials in your organization.

COMMANDMENT 2:
TREAT PROSPECTS LIKE INVESTORS

Mancuso's second principle: "Establish relationships with other people in your organization who will help you help other people get their investments back, and then some—no ifs, ands, or buts."

As Mancuso puts it, "It's all about risk reversal and getting back to zero. Treat your prospect like an investor. The more comfortable investors are when it comes to getting their initial investment back, the more likely they are to invest."

Mancuso's suggestion to CEOs is that they themselves manage the people who are directly responsible for holding on to money the company earns and saving that money. Never forget that holding on to precious capital is the result that every CEO must master. If you're working with a CEO or similarly highly placed decision-maker, make sure you frame your solution so that it addresses that fundamental concern.

My Advice

Look at what you offer as an investment that the other person is making in you and your organization. Figure out how much that investment costs—and quantify *precisely* when and *precisely* how that investment is likely to pay off for your prospect.

COMMANDMENT 3: LEARN A
LITTLE ABOUT A LOT OF STUFF

Mancuso's third principle: "Never stop learning."

Successful CEOs—especially successful *selling* CEOs—are constantly looking at the trends in their marketplace and constantly asking themselves what effect those trends will have on their customers' lives. As Mancuso puts it, "A good CEO needs to know a little about a lot." As a result, good CEOs are constantly listening to firsthand reports, reading trade magazines, attending symposiums, and so on. They empower others to get and summarize information they themselves can't track down.

CEOs who sell must be in the know. Period.

My Advice

Pick up the telephone right now, call your own organization's CEO, and ask what organizations he or she belongs to and what trade magazines he or she reads. Then call your best customer's CEO and ask that person the same two questions. Then join and subscribe.

> When evaluating an opportunity or a problem, look at all its aspects.

Twenty-four years ago, I joined an association of electrical engineers. Not because I was an electrical engineer but because I was targeting the CEO of a huge aerospace company in my territory, and *he* was a member. I joined up and volunteered to help with their next convention to be held in my town. In less than three weeks after joining, I was sitting in the living room of this CEO's home in La Jolla, California, attending the first meeting of all the members of the convention's committee. I went on to close a huge deal with the CEO I targeted.

COMMANDMENT 4: KEEP YOURSELF MOTIVATED, AND YOU'LL MOTIVATE OTHERS TO WORK WITH YOU

Mancuso's fourth principle: "You can't expect your own 'bad day' not to affect those around you in a negative way."

CEOs must be great motivators. That means they motivate themselves first—by maintaining the right mind-set and the right perspective—and then motivate others by their example. They must be a walking role model for everyone they encounter on the best ways to get over the inevitable bumps in the road that are part of each daily business journey.

My Advice

Consult the nearest mirror before your next meeting with a prospect. Does the person staring back at you look upbeat, enthusiastic, outgoing, and creatively unstoppable? If not, work on your *own* outlook first, and you'll find others falling into line behind you.

Mancuso's right—you can't afford the luxury of a bad day.

COMMANDMENT 5: SURROUND YOURSELF WITH GREAT PEOPLE

Mancuso's fifth principle: "Constantly 'interview' for new business allies, both within and outside your organization."

Any CEO who sells will tell you that it's vitally important to stay one step ahead of the organization's needs. The best way to do this is to attract and maintain relationships with the very best people.

Great leaders know how to pick team members and great business allies—and, as a general but pretty reliable rule, they never stop looking for potentially profitable new relationships. As new people prove themselves, CEOs have a way of making sure those people stick around.

My Advice

> If you can't be at your very best—take the day off. CEOs do.

The advice here is twofold. First, constantly be on the lookout for people who can help you deliver value. When you connect with someone who can, do everything you can to protect and strengthen that relationship. It's an incredibly important asset.

Second, if you're a salesperson, never forget this (easily overlooked) point: Whenever you connect with any CEO by writing a piece of correspondence, taking part in a phone conversation, leaving a voicemail message, or meeting personally, then you, my friend, are on a job interview. The position in question is "business alliance." (By the way, a remarkable number of salespeople I've trained have ended up getting job offers from companies whose CEOs they targeted as prospects.)

COMMANDMENT 6: BE PROGRESS-OBSESSED

Mancuso's sixth principle: "Make forward movement toward a goal your primary focus."

CEOs love making progress. That's one of the reasons they love things that are new—they are masters at addressing change and the opportunity it brings to move them forward toward their goals.

Joe Mancuso suggests that, whenever you bring a problem to the attention of a CEO, you make sure it sounds like it's a new problem. "Remember that reliability problem with the ABC widget production line? Well, we've got some new information on it," rather than, "That reliability problem with the ABC widget line is still plaguing us." CEOs don't have a long fuse when it comes to rehashing the same old problems.

I heard CEO after CEO make this point time and time again during my interviews: "The only real failure is making the same mistake twice."

My Advice

Be absolutely certain you're part of the solution, not part of the problem. If you can't make a unique contribution to a CEO's day, then simply don't make the call.

COMMANDMENT 7: MEASURE EVERYTHING IN (AND OUT OF) SIGHT

Mancuso's seventh principle: "Quantify, quantify, quantify."

As Mancuso puts it, "CEOs measure *everything*. It's in their blood type! That's why you've got to be able to measure the results they can expect from any of your ideas."

CEOs have a need not just to achieve measurably but to *over-achieve* measurably. Make sure you're taking this focus in your own career—and helping others to make clear, quantifiable progress toward specific goals.

My Advice

Review any important business goal—yours or someone else's—with the purpose of quantifying exactly what progress toward that goal will look like. How must results improve? What will change as a result of what you're doing? When will you be certain you're a quarter of the way there? Halfway there? Complete?

Whatever you come up with, if you can't measure it, you shouldn't be too surprised if a CEO decides not to pay much attention to it.

COMMANDMENT 8: BALANCE WORK AND FAMILY

Mancuso's eighth principle: "Ask yourself, have you ever seen a U-Haul behind a hearse?"

> CEOs love measurable results—and so should you. Get in the habit of asking directly for what you want from your team and yourself.

Successful CEOs balance their lives. Yes, they put in effort toward their goals; yes, they want results. But they know the importance of having fun with the people they love, too.

According to Mancuso, the most successful CEOs include their families in the vacation and leisure functions they sponsor. What's more, they sometimes call on those family members for help in ways you might not expect. "It's amazing what a spouse or significant other will learn at a dinner table. Strategies and networking become part of the family's job!"

My Advice

Consider this: Balance doesn't mean you're not committed; it simply means you're co-committed.

Make sure you're building time for your family and loved ones into your life. Share your hopes, dreams, and thoughts with them.

COMMANDMENT 9: DON'T GET BOGGED DOWN IN THE DETAILS

Mancuso's ninth principle: "Don't miss the forest for the trees."

Guess what? CEOs hate to write business plans.

I know we have spent a considerable amount of time on the importance of mission statements and having a vision, but you should understand that a business plan is different. It's the *details* of how a CEO will accomplish the mission and vision. And according to Mancuso, effective CEOs loathe getting distracted by details.

"CEOs know *what* needs to be done," Mancuso explains. "That's why they hate to write down all the *how* of what should happen. What I recommend to CEOs is that the plan be for everyone else—investors, suppliers, creditors, employees, and the board—and not for them. That's why they should hire someone else to write it."

My Advice

Focus on "what needs to happen"—and *why* it needs to happen—before getting distracted with the "how." When interacting with a prospect, especially a CEO, focus closely on the *what* and the *why,* and save the *how* for discussions with the members of the CEO's technical team.

> Never stop asking: *What* needs to be improved?

COMMANDMENT 10: PICK THE RIGHT RIGHT-HAND PERSON

Mancuso's tenth principle: "Be sure you get the most important personnel decision right."

CEOs who sell—and indeed, all CEOs—must pick their "first mate" carefully. A CEO's right-hand person is critically important to the success of the CEO and organization. This person may be the COO, the CFO, or the CEO's personal assistant. (Side note: Those personal assistants are sometimes among the most powerful people in the organization.)

Mancuso has a humorous but on-target way of helping a CEO select this individual. Look at the chart below.

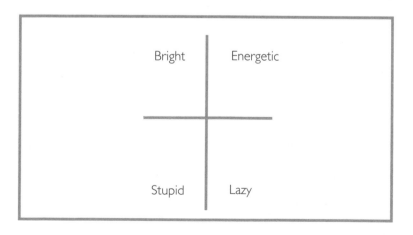

What two combinations of the traits in the chart do you think the first pick of a CEO would be? The most popular pick of CEOs that Joe Mancuso works with is "bright and energetic." But, as Mancuso points out, "that choice works for only a short time. After a while, the 'bright and energetic' player is too much of a challenge to the CEO's ego, power, control, and authority."

Mancuso continues: "There is only room for one leader—and that's the CEO."

So what's the best choice? Joe opts for "bright and lazy"— because "a smart CEO always knows how to keep the lazy person motivated and busy." (He also warns that "energetic and stupid" is a terrible choice, one that may put the whole organization at risk.)

These are oversimplifications, of course, but you see Joe's point. Most CEOs want a capable lieutenant, not a possible organizational rival.

My Advice

How you choose your own "first mate" is up to you. What's perhaps more important, if you're a salesperson targeting CEO prospects, is that you be willing to check your ego at the door whenever you make contact with a top executive. Be prepared to take direction well. Remember: CEOs love to give orders, but they love seeing people follow those orders even more.

Secrets of VITO

THINK

Memorize the ten CEO operational strategies you learned about in this chapter:

1. Create a mastermind council.
2. Treat prospects like investors.

3. Learn a little about a lot of stuff.
4. Keep yourself motivated.
5. Surround yourself with great people.
6. Be progress-obsessed.
7. Measure everything.
8. Balance work and family.
9. Don't get bogged down in the details.
10. Pick the right right-hand person.

SELL

Think of your most important target CEO. Now rethink your next meeting or conversation with this person, given what you've learned about the list above. How many of the ten priorities can you address *directly* with what you offer or propose?

TAKE ACTION

Model each of these operating principles as follows:

> Make a list of ten of the top sales performers in your organization—or ten top-notch noncompeting organizations in your sales territory. Now organize a monthly in-person, telephone, or "chatroom" discussion.

> Make sure you understand the total cost of implementing your products, services, and solutions. This price might be much higher than the list price of what you sell. Once you know that number, calculate the return to your best customer—and be ready to discuss it. This is much more honest and accurate than anything your competition will provide your prospect.

> If you haven't already done so, find out what organizations your CEO belongs to and what trade magazines he or she reads. Then call your best customer's CEO and ask that person the same two questions. Then join and subscribe to the organizations that seem like the best investments of your time and energy.

- Consult the nearest mirror before your next meeting with a prospect. Does the person staring back at you look upbeat, enthusiastic, outgoing, and creatively unstoppable?

- Constantly be on the lookout for people who can help you deliver value to your prospects and customers, and when you connect with someone who can, do everything you can to protect and strengthen that relationship. If you sell freight forwarding services, get to know the top people in the custom container business.

- Be absolutely certain that you're an important part of the CEO's solution—and not part of the CEO's problem. If you can't make a unique contribution to a CEO's day, then simply don't make the call.

- For each and every sales situation you're engaged in, ask yourself: *How* must results improve? *What* will change as a result of what I am offering? *When* will I be able to be certain I'm (a quarter, half, or three-quarters) of the way there?

- Put in a massive effort toward your goals, but know the importance of having fun, too. Consider this: Balance doesn't mean that you're not committed; it simply means that you're co-committed. If your "cup" becomes empty, you can't fill anyone else's. Translation: Take time to charge your batteries.

- When interacting with a prospective CEO, focus on "what needs to happen"—and *why* it needs to happen—before getting distracted with *how* it needs to happen.

- If you're a salesperson targeting CEO prospects, be willing to check your ego at the door so you can become one of the CEO's "right-hand people."

17

---

*"Advice is what we ask for when we already know
the answer but we wish we didn't."*

—ERICA JONG

CEOs TELL
IT ALL

J oe Sugarman is the face behind the internationally known
BluBlocker sunglasses. He is also responsible for bringing to
market more than 100 other successful consumer and business
products.

As CEOs who sell go, they don't get much more qualified than
Sugarman. He is a bestselling marketing author; he is also a master at selling what he markets. He now earns more for a one-
hour speech than many of his successful business peers earn in a
month.

Why would corporations pay so much for his words of wis-
dom? Because what he has to say can transform an ordinary sales
message into a powerful, compelling reason to buy. I managed to
interview Sugarman for an hour while he was on a short layover
between his beautiful ranch on the island of Maui and a trip to

Europe. What you're about to learn will, I believe, change the way you approach and sell to CEOs and other high-level prospects, no matter what it is you're selling.

One word of caution: Sugarman doesn't have time for negative thinking, and neither do you. To get the most out of this chapter, you may want to remove the word "can't" from your vocabulary. Just drop the apostrophe and the "t," and you'll do just fine.

SUGARMAN'S LAWS

According to Sugarman, marketing is an exact science. Sales, in his world, is a blend of an exact science and art form. Actually, if you take the time to read Sugarman's bestseller *Triggers* (Delstar Publishing), and I urge you to do so, you'll find he has identified no fewer than 30 reasons/triggers that can make your offer irresistible to your prospects. I asked Sugarman to talk about the most powerful motivating factors for people who want to get deals moving with CEO prospects. Here's what he passed along.

Sugarman's First Law: "People Buy from People They Like"

Seems obvious enough, doesn't it? Then how come so many salespeople seem to come off as downright obnoxious? (That may sound like an extreme judgment, but think back to the past five or six conversations you've had with telemarketers, and I think you'll see my point.)

Sugarman's advice here is simple and straightforward: Do what it takes to be likable to individuals outside your family and immediate circle of friends. We're not suggesting you behave outside your standards of integrity or conform to habits that contradict your culture. What Sugarman strongly suggests is that you build personal rapport with your prospects quickly, starting with your first interaction. Don't wait until you meet someone face-to-face to start this process. Treat every interaction as an appreciable opportunity to make contact and improve the relationship with your target CEO. In Sugarman's words, "You must establish integrity and credibility in an honest way." This means demonstrating that you're the kind of person who does what's promised. Demonstrate this early and often.

If you give compliments, make sure they're sincere. If you make contact by means of the written word, be sure what you write is targeted directly and specifically to the individual. And at any expense, make totally sure you sign whatever it is that you send. I just received a letter from a high-net-worth financial planner touting its attention to detail that wasn't even signed.

Sugarman's Second Law: "Raise the Objection Yourself"

> Don't partici-
> pate in the
> fool's game of
> "mirroring" a
> prospective
> CEO's person-
> ality or physical
> posture.

Every single product that's ever been manufactured, and every service that's ever been offered, has had its fair share of flaws. So the question is, What are you as a salesperson going to do when those flaws are pointed out to you?

Prior to interviewing Joe Sugarman, I thought my 28 years of sales experience had taught me everything I needed to know about handling objections. Was I ever wrong! What follows is the most creative objection-handling technique I've ever heard. If you do nothing but implement this one idea when you interact with CEOs, you will easily and instantly earn back the purchase price of this book several hundred and perhaps thousands of times over.

Sugarman recommends that instead of "burying" the disadvantages in your product, service, or solution, you bring those disadvantages up on your own initiative.

Stop right now. Go back and read that last paragraph again.

In other words, don't try to cover anything up. Ever. Take your product's weakest feature and shine the spotlight on it yourself. "It's amazing," he observes, "how bringing up the disadvantage first is not only disarming but also a great way to reduce the negative impact the disadvantage has on your offer."

Sugarman speaks from experience. He's tried this, and it works. I (now) speak from experience. I've tried this, and it works. I know it sounds pretty crazy at first, this idea really does have amazing implications.

Here's why you should give this seemingly stupid idea an honest try: You'll never really be able to fool your prospect. As Sugarman explains, "The trust and respect you get from a CEO by raising your greatest weakness will lower their defense mechanisms, and so they'll be prepared to receive the real benefits and advantages of what you've got to offer."

There is, of course, a sizable downside risk to Sugarman's tactic. As he points out, "If you don't raise the *real* objection that your prospects have in their minds, then you're totally wasting your time, and you'll raise the CEO's suspicion that you're really trying to cover something up."

> Raising a serious objection can actually build trust and confidence from your target CEO.

How do you find out what objections potential prospects may have? There doesn't seem to be much of an alternative to real experience. If you don't have that yet, take a customer out to lunch and ask for the straight scoop on how your product or service is performing. If you don't yet have any customers, ask your marketing department what they've learned. Learn the *honest-to-goodness* shortcomings of what you're selling, and you'll be able to master this tactic.

My true story: I've been trying to sell a mountain retreat for the past ten months. Second homes are not a hot item now, and furthermore, this little piece of paradise happens to be a good hour and a half drive east of downtown San Diego, California. Basically, it's out of the way and a pain in the neck to get to. Everyone who has looked at the house expressed their concern about the drive. I ran an ad to drum up some prospects to show my listing agent that he needed to get more creative to sell the house. The headline of my ad read, "Second home buyers! Why should you drive an hour and a half?" The balance of my ad was chock-full of the benefits of a secluded hideaway: peace and quiet, abundant nature, clear skies and clean air, a place to renew and re-energize. Pose the objection, then handle it. It's simply brilliant.

I've since adapted this incredibly powerful idea to several interactions with CEOs and gotten great results. Thanks, Joe!

Now—what's *your* success story going to be?

Sugarman's Third Law: "Be Ready to Resolve Any Objection"

You must—repeat, must—resolve all the objections that you raise, and you must be totally prepared to answer the ones that CEOs may happen to come up with on their own. So practice ahead of time. Sugarman's own experience tells him that the more experienced you are at objection raising, the less experienced you'll have to be at objection handling. He urges you to ask questions to confirm the true dimensions of the objection.

"You won't be caught off-guard as often if you follow my objection-raising technique," he explains. True enough, but to be on the safe side, take a look at what four other CEOs have to say about handling objections. (It's no surprise that they basically mirror Sugarman's process.)

> *View each objection as a request for additional information. But don't give that information—at least, not right away. Your initial response to any objection should be a question!*
> —Keith McCumber, CEO, Daylight Systems Inc.

> *If an objection catches you off guard... don't answer it! Ask your prospect for their patience and then ask for their advice on how to answer the challenge.*
> —Bob Palmisano, CEO, MacroChem

Any objection is an invitation to sell. Take it, rephrase it,
and look at it however you need to—but whatever you do,
don't attack it!

—Doug Simon, CEO, Mobility Elevator & Lift Company

Bringing your prospect to a "no" sooner rather than later is
a great way to begin the real relationship. It's never too soon
to ask your prospect if they will buy from you.

—Fred W. Green, CEO

As you can see, defining an objection as an "object" to warrant further consideration, and dialogue is a great way to begin using a successful CEO's approach to objection resolution.

Sugarman's Fourth Law: "Develop a Satisfaction Conviction Statement"

A satisfaction conviction statement is to a guarantee as a Pinto is an Aston Martin. It's a way of taking the game (or the ride) to a whole different level.

Ask yourself:
What will be
your target
CEO's likely
response to
what you say?

How many times have you seen or heard words like "free trial period" and "satisfaction guaranteed"? Thousands? Millions? How many times have those words actually prompted you to take a second look at the offer in question? Hardly ever, right?

According to Joe Sugarman, a satisfaction *conviction* takes the idea of a guarantee to an entirely different level. As usual, Sugarman explains it better than I can:

If my prospect, after reading or hearing my offer, thinks,
"They really must believe in their product," or "How can they do
that?" or "They're really going to get ripped off by customers
who will take advantage of them"—then I know I've got it right.

A satisfaction conviction statement is a promise to a prospect that elicits such a reaction. You can effectively apply this idea to almost every product or service, even memberships or subscriptions.

Sugarman uses a real example to make this point. "When faced with selling subscriptions to a consumer's newsletter," he explains, "I noticed that when I lowered the price of the subscription, my response rate went up marginally. But when I changed just the satisfaction conviction, the response rate *doubled*. I received over 100 percent more orders!"

Sugarman knows that if your guarantee is linked to a limited time (like 30 days), the prospect will be concerned they may not use the product fully or find any flaws in that period of time. Extend the period *indefinitely*, and you disarm the potential objection and replace it with commitment from the prospect.

> Don't make your satisfaction conviction too outrageous. CEOs know that you must make a profit on your sale.

Consider these examples:

Mr. CEO, if you are not satisfied with the information in our newsletter, you can cancel your subscription at any time for a full refund.

You've heard something like that a thousand times, right? Now compare that wimpy "guarantee" to this satisfaction conviction statement:

Mr. CEO, if you are not satisfied with the information in our newsletter, you can cancel your subscription at any time for a full refund. Even after it expires.

Take a moment right now and script out a "satisfaction conviction" statement for your product, service, or solution. Do this even if you don't have the power to implement the solution; then bounce it off the right people within your organization. At the very least, they'll be impressed with your ingenuity. And who knows? They might even let you implement your idea, especially if you show your own CEO this chapter.

Before we move on to law number 5, consider this true story. I travel the nation giving public sales seminars as part of my popular "Selling to VITO, the Very Important Top Officer" program. The system teaches salespeople how to get appointments with difficult-to-reach, top decision-makers. During these events, I sell my products (audiotapes and web-based learning) to the audience.

I used to get 5 percent of the audience to invest in my products. While in Houston, I tested Sugarman's satisfaction conviction principle by telling my audience that if they weren't happy with my products, they could get their entire investment back—and they could *keep* the product, give it to a friend, or sell it on e-Bay. Someone in the audience asked, "How long is that guarantee good for?" I responded, "The rest of your life."

Guess what happened? Ninety-eight out of the 480 people in the audience invested in my package. That's 20 percent. I've been using Sugarman's strategy for six months now with great results, and no one yet has wanted to return the package.

A word of caution: Don't make outlandish claims you can't back up. If you know your product, service, or solution can't measure up, don't set yourself up for a fall.

Sugarman's Fifth Law: "Greed Works"

Yeah, yeah, yeah. I know. I've been reading the headlines, too. That word "greed" definitely has a negative feel to it. When Sugarman first mentioned this rule to me, I have to admit, I raised my eyebrows. I felt better, though, when he explained exactly what he meant: "Greed isn't a technique that can be employed all the time. But it should be recognized as an effective element that, when properly employed, is a great trigger for making a sale because it plays on practically everybody's weakness."

Sugarman is very committed on this score. He continues: "Whenever you increase the value of whatever it is that you sell, you'll almost always end up with an easier sale." When you increase the value and then lower the price, you'll begin to appeal to the greed factor. Continue to add value and lower the price, and you'll end up with a sale that requires less justification and less logic. Continue this process, and you'll create an enhanced emotional desire for your product, service, or solution. Of course, if the price goes low enough, all sense of logic will be thrown out the window. According to Sugarman, at this point, the purchase/investment becomes completely emotional. You may also lose money in the process. The key here is, as any good CEO knows, margins must be your primary consideration when it comes to lowering your prices.

Help your target CEOs conclude that they've met their need to get more than they actually paid for.

Let me add a cautionary note. If you go too high with the value and too low with the price, your credibility may become questionable in the eyes of the prospect CEO, who will start asking, "What's wrong with this picture?"

Secrets of VITO

THINK

CEOs like to make powerful statements. They also like to use industrial-strength marketing and sales tactics. Here are four key ideas that CEOs who sell embrace daily; you should get your arms around them, too.

1. *People buy from people they like.* This is not the same as "being like" someone. Make sure you never, ever try to "mirror" a target CEO.

2. *Raise your worst objection yourself.* Total disclosure is essential if you hope to build credibility.

3. *Be ready to resolve any objection.* Think ahead. What other questions/objections might this target CEO bring up? Remember: CEOs like answers to their questions.

4. *Develop a satisfaction conviction statement.* Use the conviction statement as a risk-reversal strategy.

SELL

Ask yourself, What can I do on or before my next sales call to make sure that my target CEO not only doesn't miss out on anything but also comes away feeling as though he or she is getting more value than anticipated? (See Take Action below for some ideas on this.)

TAKE ACTION

Here's a three-step exercise that will help you convey, in a powerful way, everything you deliver to your customers.

Step #1. Write down all the value that you deliver to your prospects and customers that you *don't* charge for. This list should include all the items that you deliver that don't show up on your invoice. For instance: expedited delivery, help desk, preinstallation consulting, installation and setup, warranty periods, first-year service, extended service hours, optional equipment, etc. Write your value down on a separate sheet of paper; list at least five items.

Step #2. Attach a dollar amount to each of these items of added value. In other words, what would it cost your prospect if he or she had to pay for all that stuff you typically deliver *without* charging? Make sure your estimates are realistic.

Step #3. Include a breakdown of the aforementioned value and price in your next ten proposals or presentations. As the prospect understands the value that you deliver, you can begin to appeal to greed by *reducing* the overall price you're actually recommending. You can do this with statements like these: "On this slide, we've listed the price for each of the added-value initiatives that we provide to our customers free of charge. We wanted you to know that it's because of this value that our price and cost of ownership is actually X percent below that of our nearest competitor."

18

BECOMING A
TRUSTED ADVISOR

The most successful CEOs and corporate leaders are all about *long-term commitment to positive change.* They surround themselves with people they can trust, people they believe can help them make that long-term commitment a way of life for the organization. The question is, how do you become one of those people?

Let's focus, for a moment, on the model of the large public company. Let's assume that's the kind of firm you're targeting.

If you picture a two-step ladder, with the highest one being the position of the CEO, the next level down is the person or people who "direct" the work force. (This group excludes, of course, the board of directors and the CEO's personal assistant, who can be powerful players, indeed.)

> You're on a job interview whenever you make contact with a CEO. When CEOs decide to do business with your company—consider yourself on the payroll.

These "directors" may have titles such as: president, divisional president, county manager, or general manager, to name a few. They are held responsible for the implementation of the vision and for meeting (or, preferably, exceeding) the expectations of the CEO.

As Joe Mancuso, CEO and founder of the CEO Club, sees it, the job of the best "directors" in the organization is also to be a trusted advisor—a consultant of sorts—to the person at the top. "Direct reports need to speak the truth as often as possible to the leader," Mancuso observes. (This principle can be applied to a corporate leader at other levels than CEO, of course.)

If we take Mancuso's advice and apply it to our sales efforts and our interactions with corporate leaders, we see that we can become a "director" of sorts to the person we're targeting—a trusted consultant or confidant. In fact, our mobility and autonomy as salespeople give us the freedom of movement that many "real" directors don't have.

A TRUE STORY

Jonathan Crain was one of two presidents to the CEO at a major telecommunications company. (That is, he was a "director" to that CEO.) A while back, I was conducting my "Selling to VITO™" training seminars at all their branch offices across America. After two years of conducting the program (during which time they realized the results I had guaranteed), I got a call from Crain asking for an in-person meeting.

So it was that I flew to Ryebrook, New York, and took a seat in Crain's corner office. I thought I was ready for anything, but I wasn't ready for what Crain asked me to do that morning.

"Tony," he said, "at this point you've met more of my salespeople than I have. I want you to take your time and tell me what they're thinking. I want you to report back to me. How do they feel about what we're asking them to do?"

I realized, at that moment, that in that two-year period of delivering results, I had earned the right to act as a trusted consultant to my contact. In other words, Crain was a "director" to the CEO, and I was a "director" to Crain.

Here's the kicker: Before I left Crain's office, I said, "I have an idea. Jonathan, would you like for me to develop a similar seminar for your sales managers— to show them how to do the kind of digging that I'll be doing for you?"

"Great idea," he said. "Do it."

Notice the two most important elements of this story.

> The strength and loyalty of any business relationship will always be proportional to the value it delivers over time.

1. *I was trusted.* Although I wasn't aware of it, the director— in this case, the president (Jonathan Crain)—was watching my activities. At the time he needed me, he called upon my knowledge of his entire sales organization.

2. *I strengthened the business relationship with additional services.* Once it was obvious I had the knowledge and ability to act as a "consultant" and "confidant," I was given the opportunity to provide even greater value to my customer with my seminar for managers.

BECOME A CONSULTANT TO EVERY CEO

If you pattern your value after the most trusted directors in the CEO's organization, you'll be on your way to becoming a true consultative salesperson. Here's how to make that happen:

> Learn to share your opinions with CEOs— tactfully—when asked to do so. Don't take sides or make accusations.

- *Pick a specialty.* If you are selling accounting systems, become the street-smart equivalent of an MBA and know the ins and outs of the life

Introduce your team early on in the sales process. CEOs like to know who's responsible for what.

of a CFO. The fastest way to do this is for you to know your own organization's CFO. And once you've picked a specialty, master the ability to speak about it concisely. Joel Ronning, CEO of Digital River, says his first-string team must be "close to the bone." What does that mean? To get on that team, you have to know your stuff and get to the point. "I'll meet with anyone," Ronning says, "who can quickly prove to me that they know how their products can benefit me." Ronning places special emphasis on the word *quickly.* "I'll give them 15 seconds to make their point. I don't have the time to 'untangle' their message."

- *Voice your opinion.* When a CEO or other corporate leader asks you your opinion, give it. Be ready to give your opinion when asked. Emil Wang, CEO of Latitude Communications, asks this question of salespeople who call on him: "What do you want me to do?" (He chuckled when he told me he usually gets an empty stare or silence on the telephone line in response to this question.)

- *Show up.* In my experience, 80 percent of winning trust and becoming a consultant in the eyes of a CEO is simply *being there when you're supposed to* and *doing exactly what you've promised.* I am talking about your physical and emotional presence. The CEO must *feel* your belief in and conviction for the work you're doing. Cash Nickerson, CEO and founder of Team America, says, "Endurance is by far the single most important element that a team must have. I can keep them focused, but they must keep their own momentum." Translation: To get on the CEO's team, keep your commitments and provide your own momentum.

- *Bring a team of experts to the table.* Successful "directors" have resources behind them to get the job done—people who are energized and directed. I'll quote Nickerson again here: "Animals hunt in packs—because a team is more effective than one individual. Scouts—like CEOs—are loners. Once they find the opportunity, they call in the pack to get the job done." Moral: Make sure you've got the right pack behind you to complete the assignment.

- *Never stop adding value.* "I can't be successful without you!" That's the mantra you want every corporate leader you do business with to embrace. The way to make sure that happens is to make yourself and your products, services, and solutions absolutely irreplaceable. You can't do that if you don't know your own product or service inside and out. Consider what Bob Posten, CEO of Landis Strategy & Innovation, has to say on this score. "You must become a user of whatever it is that you're selling. Never stop asking yourself these critical questions: How would my customer use this? And how can I make my offer more valuable to customers when they do use this?"

A LITTLE BIT OF LOYALTY GOES A LONG WAY

The most important part of becoming a trusted advisor may well be your ability to establish, maintain, and grow business relationships that have loyalty as their centerpiece. How do you win loyalty? By offering it, of course.

Here are just a few closing comments on loyalty from the CEOs I interviewed.

> *Always put more of yourself at risk than you're asking others to ante up with.*
>
> —Jay Rodgers, Chairman of the Board, Smart Start Inc.

> *People at the top hire coaches. Become one!*
>
> —Bob Posten, CEO, Landis Strategy & Innovation

Remember: Trusted advisors don't appear out of nowhere—they earn their role over time.

> *Don't try too hard—if you do, people will have a hard time*
> *trusting you.*
>
> —Jennifer Ash, CEO, Tomco Tool & Die

Secrets of VITO

THINK

Long-term commitment to positive change is a popular CEO mantra. It's not surprising, then, that so many CEOs surround themselves with people they believe can help them make long-term commitment to constructive change a way of life for the organization.

How do you become one of those people? Read on.

SELL

> ➤ *Be the best "you" that you can be.* Whenever you send a correspondence, make an in-person visit, place a telephone call, or leave a voice-mail message, consider yourself to be on a job interview. (You are.)
> ➤ *Pick a specialty.* Become the street-smart equivalent of an MBA; get to know the ins and outs of whatever niche you happen to be selling to.
> ➤ *Make it free.* Make it obvious that you have the knowledge and ability to act as a "consultant" and "confidant"—without the fees that are normally associated with that type of service.
> ➤ *Voice your opinion (when asked to do so).* When a CEO or other corporate leader asks you your opinion, give it. (Make sure, however, that you don't point fingers.)
> ➤ *Show up.* My estimate is that 80 percent of winning trust and becoming a consultant in the eyes of a CEO lies simply in being where you're supposed to be when you're supposed to be there and doing exactly what you've promised.

> ➤ *Bring a team of experts to the table.* Make sure you've got the team behind you to complete the assignment!

> ➤ *Never stop adding value.* Make sure you and your products, services, and solutions become absolutely irreplaceable. Continually ask yourself questions like these: "How would my customer use this?" "How can I make what I offer more valuable to my customers?"

TAKE ACTION

Understand that the trusted-advisor relationship only comes about *after* you've delivered results for a significant period of time. With that in mind, identify the three *most likely* candidates in your own customer base with whom you could develop this kind of relationship. Then establish at least three action steps based on the ideas in this chapter for each of these people.

PART 7

CEOs Teach You

19

CEOs Teach
Us to Listen

I didn't learn the true importance of listening until I was well into my career as a salesperson. I was sitting in the office of the CEO and president of The Robertson Company, Grady Robertson. That afternoon, Grady gave me a lesson in listening I'll never forget. But before I can tell you about what I learned, I have to tell you about my ears.

After a tour in the U.S. Navy, my hearing was compromised; I had loud and annoying noises in my ears constantly. They were sort of like permanent "buzzing" and "gushing" sound effects. The bottom line: I'm not deaf, but I do have limited hearing. When I got out of the Navy as a young man, I decided that wearing large, visible hearing aids behind my already-prominent ears wasn't really what I had in mind. So I simply put up with the weird noises and decided I was going to learn how to read lips.

> Want to show someone you're really listening? Pretend you're deaf and just read their lips; watch the person's face intently and hang on every word.

Now, as it turns out, lip-reading is hard work. I mastered it, but I also learned it takes intense concentration. At the end of a day of lip-reading as a computer salesperson, you're mentally exhausted. At the same time, I found that having a hearing impairment that requires you to read lips isn't exactly a handicap if you're pursuing a career in sales.

Think about it: When you lip-read, you must *watch* what's being said at the same time you *listen* to what's being said. That means you must look intently and pay close attention to the person who happens to be doing the talking.

All of which brings me back to Grady Robertson. When I first met him, I was still lip-reading. I closed the sale while I was still lip-reading. But on the afternoon I'm telling you about now, I was meeting him for the first time *after* I'd been fitted with a new, almost-invisible set of hearing aids. They were amazing. They fit right into my ears, and I didn't have to lip-read anymore. I could actually hear what people were saying without watching them.

On all my previous meetings with Robertson, I had had to sit at the edge of my chair, lean forward, and watch his every move with incredible attention. I couldn't let anything distract me. I never let anything take my eyes from Robertson's face. If someone walked by his open office door I couldn't turn to look. I couldn't afford to miss a word like "if," "but," or "maybe." Those can be pretty important words when you're trying to sell a computer system.

On this afternoon, though, when Robertson summoned me to his office to discuss some problems he was having with the system we'd shipped him, I noticed that my seat was a lot more comfortable than it had seemed last time. Perhaps this had something to do with the fact that I was sitting all the way back on the cushion and not on the very edge, the better to make out every movement of Robertson's face and lips.

Robertson began to tell me about the problems he was having with the new system. He said, "Tony, two of my new terminals aren't working." (I pulled the account file from my briefcase and thought to myself, What's so new about that? I bet they were shipped without the crossover circuit modification. No problem.) Robertson continued: "Tony—we didn't get the right manuals with the system console." I stared up at the ceiling and thought, Sounds like the shipping department was short-handed again. Then I noticed Robertson's personal assistant standing outside his office with a maintenance person setting up a ladder; she was pointing up at a ceiling tile, and he was adjusting his flashlight and tool belt.

All of a sudden, Robertson stopped in the middle of his next complaint, which had to do with an incorrect cable size, and stared at me.

Then he said, "Tony, you're not listening to what I'm saying. You haven't even looked at me since you sat down."

> Here's a prediction: Your sales results will soar if you listen at least three times as much as you talk.

Talk about shocked. I suddenly had the worst case of cotton-mouth. I told the truth. "Grady, I'm sorry—I just got a new pair of hearing aids, and I guess I'm letting them do the listening for me."

At that precise moment, Grady Robertson gave me my greatest lesson on listening: "Tony," he said, "please take your hearing aids out. I liked it when you had to sit at the edge of that chair and watch my every move. What I am saying is critically important to our business relationship and the success of my company. I want your undivided attention."

My hands trembled as I removed my hearing aids and put them into my pocket. Robertson grinned slightly and began at the top of his complaint list all over again. I listened like I had before, sitting at the edge of my chair, concentrating on his every move.

The moral: If you're going to meet with a CEO, *you've got to listen like you're lip-reading.* If you do, you'll send an important message: "You're the most important person in the universe to me right now." That's what *they* want to hear.

SOME THOUGHTS ON LISTENING FROM CEOs

If you're working with a top decision-maker, you'll want to know how they look at this whole listening issue so you don't have to get a traumatizing "listening lesson" in quite the way I did. Here then are lessons from the top. Listen up!

> *"The fastest way to empower anyone is to listen!"*

As you listen to a CEO, ask yourself: Why is this CEO telling me this?

Mike Bowman has never had the title of CEO, but he has had 600 direct reports who in turn had more than 50,000 people reporting to them. Mike Bowman has never had to be concerned with profit-and-loss statements, but he has been responsible for hundreds of millions of dollars in capital equipment and other assets. In 35 years, Bowman worked his way up the chain of command in the U.S. Navy, first as a combat pilot in Vietnam, then air wing commander of a battle group, which flew combat missions during Desert Storm, and later as an aide to the Secretary of the Navy at the Pentagon. Currently, he is a consultant to the U.S. Navy on public affairs.

Thoughts on Listening from Mike Bowman

Getting launched from the flight deck of the USS America will get your attention. You better have been listening to the preflight briefing.

The fastest way to empower anyone is to listen to them— as long as the person is talking about something that's important to the mission at hand.

In my entire career, I've only had to ground one pilot. Why? Because he didn't listen.

When you're in command, you must have total confidence in your people—you must relinquish responsibilities and let them do their job. The only way to have a successful mission is to be sure that they listened to their orders and have understood them.

When I listen to someone, I constantly ask myself, "How can I help this person make their mission a success and not a statistic?"

TAKING CONTROL OF THE CONVERSATION

Peter Shea, owner and CEO of Entrepreneur Media, worked his way up the corporate ladder in an interesting way. At 23, he was selling copiers door to door for AB Dick. By 1972, he was CEO of the largest copier sorting equipment supplier in the world. He purchased *Entrepreneur* magazine in 1987 and has turned it into a top-flight media conglomerate.

Although Shea is a master at checking his own ego at the door before he makes a sales call, he's not shy about taking control during a conversation. Because the corporation is "his baby," he can make outrageous statements and claims that can turn a conversation and sales situation around. "I'll ask a very direct question," he says, "fully knowing that I may not like the answer."

> Name dropping works well, if you're sure the person you're dropping the name on is fond of the name you're dropping.

Peter Shea's Advice on Getting CEOs to Listen

Shea's advice to salespeople is as quick as the race cars he drives.

Get to the point as quickly as possible, be straightforward, and don't act like you know me if you don't.

Get your prospect to feel comfortable with you, and they'll open up. Get your prospect to feel like you're listening to them, and they'll buy from you.

WORKING WITH A BIG NET

> When you're in a conversation with a CEO, don't worry about what you're going to say next. Instead, think about what the other person wants to get from this interaction.

If you take the time right now and call Comfort Direct, you may just get in touch with the CEO, Kevin Dyevich. As we've seen, he's no stranger to picking up the telephone to handle customer calls. "You need to stay in touch with everyone. Never remove yourself from your market."

Dyevich is a master at listening—to his customers and to everybody else. He never lets himself fall into the "this sounds familiar" trap. "It's like fishing. Only you need to throw a bigger net. The bigger the net, the more information you'll gain during any conversation." Dyevich sees information as the key to building the largest manufacturer of high-quality mattresses.

Advice on Listening from Kevin Dyevich

I keep my listening on track during conversations by taking the "golden rule" one step further: "Do unto others as they want to be done unto." That's the only way to have a conversation that's meaningful and that takes him one step closer to the right goal.

CEOs AND LISTENING—WHAT YOU CAN EXPECT

Be honest. Some CEOs are great listeners, and some aren't. Here are the "good and the bad" listening habits that I personally observed among CEOs and the individuals they surround themselves with. I'm focusing on the "challenge" areas first because hey—you need to know what you're likely to be up against.

Four Bad Listening Habits of CEOs

1. *Never take notes.* Some CEOs are so used to having an assistant that they seem to have forgotten how to write.

2. *Multitask.* "Go ahead—I'm listening. I've just got to sign these checks and make a quick call." At least 25 percent of the CEOs I interviewed were doing more than one thing while they were talking to me.

3. *Flunk at feelings.* CEOs are so driven to success that they often fail to understand the feelings of others; it's hard for them to empathize with the situations and emotions of other people.

4. *Rarely restate.* Only on certain occasions have I heard a CEO restate a question that was asked. CEOs usually launch headfirst into their own response, and often don't even wait for the person posing the question to finish.

> Don't volunteer words that CEOs are searching for. Let them sweat it out. What they come up with will be better than what you would have suggested, anyway.

Four Good Listening Habits of CEOs

1. *Have no fear.* Good CEOs aren't afraid to ask a question for clarification. You'll remember Howard Putnam, past CEO of Southwest Airlines and Braniff Airlines. He regularly showed up at the places where he was least likely to be found. Why? Because he wasn't shy about asking questions or being asked questions. In other words, he knew he didn't have all the answers, and he was self-assured and confident enough in his quest for knowledge (asking questions). Putnam came across as someone who was *interested* in others—and his listening skills had a lot to do with that.

2. *Listen to everybody.* Successful CEOs don't judge the importance of what's being said by the uniform of the person saying it. CEOs will listen to people at all levels of business stature, from the custodian to the chairperson of the board.

   Dock Houk, the CEO of the National Heritage Foundation, recently wrote a book with a convict. Why?

Because he decided the lesson he and his co-author could teach potential lawbreakers could have a profound and positive effect on society. He never could have completed the book if he'd had deep-rooted ideas about status that kept him from connecting with someone from a different social background.

3. *Don't overreact.* Successful CEOs learn how to maintain their cool during conversations, and so should you. If you let the emotional content of any communication get to you, you won't be able to listen effectively—or settle on the right course of action. It's all in your attitude, says Jay Rodgers, chairman of the board, Smart Start, Inc. Rodgers advises: "Read between the lines, and always play with your cards facing up. When listening, constantly ask yourself, "How can I help this person win?" Constantly ask yourself, "Is this person's body language matching what this person is saying?"

4. *Don't assume they have all the facts.* CEOs who have mastered the highest levels of listening never say to themselves while they are listening, "This sounds like such and such; I don't have to pay attention." The most successful CEOs give the person doing the talking the power by asking focused questions and letting the other person speak.

> Effective CEO communication trait: Focus on the content of the other person's message—not the externals.

Secrets of VITO

THINK

"The fastest way to empower anyone is to listen."

This quote comes to us from Mike Bowman, Veteran Navy fighter pilot and Desert Storm squadron leader. Bowman points out that listening to a target CEO is as important as listening to a flight briefing before a sortie. When CEOs talk, we need to listen intently; when we do so, we get their experience and insight, and they feel power and authority. That's a two-way victory.

SELL

Follow the four golden rules when it comes to communicating with people in your target organization.

1. *Have no fear.* CEOs aren't afraid to ask a question for clarification; you shouldn't be, either. When you ask intelligent questions, you'll come across as someone who is interested and engaged.

2. *Listen to everybody.* Understand that good information can come from anywhere in the organization.

3. *Don't overreact.* Successful CEOs learn how to maintain their cool during conversations—and so should you. If you let the emotional content of any communication get to you, you won't be able to listen effectively—or settle on the right course of action.

4. *Don't assume anything.* The most effective CEOs look around corners and "peek" behind doors—just in case.

TAKE ACTION

➤ Master the art of interrupting without interrupting.

➤ Understand that *your* listening skills have to be excellent and the CEO's listening skills are likely to be spotty. These facts carry some interesting implications.

> Maintaining EBS with a CEO is a tricky business that often requires a strange kind of conversation management that involves interrupting without *actually* interrupting. You can master this skill by reviewing the points below—and practicing them at your next meeting.

> Basically, CEOs know how to influence the outcome of any conversation by means of a simple four-step process: listen, interrupt, ask, and listen. I've seen hundreds of CEOs employ this in their communications with their own team members. The pattern is always the same: First, the CEO listens for a very brief moment; then the CEO interrupts with an observation or an issue, which invariably leads to a very focused question. Then the CEO listens and gives her/his advice.

> Believe it or not, you can practice an adapted version of this "listen, interrupt, ask, and listen" pattern without seeming too overbearing. To find out how, look at the following (real) sales conversation I had recently with a CEO.

CEO: *Investors are quick to judge and are jaded by technology that relates to telecommunications and networks. We're at a standstill with our expansion funding.*

(CEO now takes a breath before continuing with the woes of venture capital availability and its consequences on corporate vision.)

I interrupt while CEO breathes and ask: *Let me ask you. What level of funding over what period of time would make your expansion plans turn into a reality?* (This question cuts to the chase of the real issue.)

CEO: *Twenty million over a three-year period. With add-on options at the halfway point if we need it.*

Me: *Want my opinion?*

CEO: *What's that?*

Now the CEO will listen intently to my creative ideas about providing return and investment protection for all investors. Note that I *didn't* simply stop the CEO midsentence and say, "Hold on—I've got a great idea."

Here are several short interruption statements that I have witnessed CEOs using to interrupt a conversation. I've rewritten each one (shown in italicized print) in a way that will make it easy for any non-CEO to use the same basic "interruption" (OK, statement delivered while the CEO stops for a split second) in a conversation. Wait for 'em to take a breath—then get your "interruption" statement in!

> Let me give you my opinion. *Would you like my opinion?*
> Let me give you some feedback. *Are you looking for some feedback?*
> Let me ask you a quick question. *Could I ask you a quick question to validate what I just heard you say?*
> I want you to consider… *Would you consider…?*
> I want you to take a moment and consider… *Would you take a moment and consider…?*
> Look at this. *Consider looking at this… That reminds me of… You just sounded like… You sound as if you…*

Practice and master the art of interrupting without interrupting and put it into your own words, and you'll be able to get the *right* information from the CEO you're working with.

For additional information and worksheets, visit:
www.CEOsellingtips.com
Click on: "Get Info"
Locate and download Chapter 19.

20

"Honest disagreement is often a good sign of progress."

—GANDHI

CEOs Share Ideas on Negotiating

In my interviews with CEOs, I got the best advice on negotiating from the people I considered to be the wisest and most experienced. This is not surprising. Let's look briefly at the most profound—and subtle—traits for wise negotiating, as practiced by the men and women at the top.

> Don't confuse being wise with acting like a wise guy. The latter will kill a deal faster than you can imagine.

WISE NEGOTIATING TRAIT 1: PICK YOUR BATTLES CAREFULLY

CEOs who sell and negotiate successfully know that sometimes even the most valiant fight may not be worth the potential loss it entails. They know it's up to them to assign value to the campaign they decide to take on or decline—not outside forces like sales vice presidents or prospective customers. In other words, good CEOs are more likely than most other businesspeople to "walk" when they sense there will be no alternative to a bad deal. They don't negotiate a deal just to be able to say they've negotiated something.

Karin Bellintoni, CEO of I-Mark (the company that specializes in "permission-based" voice-mail messaging systems), puts it this way: "I'll only negotiate with people who can hear my message."

WISE NEGOTIATING TRAIT 2: NO LOOSE ENDS

Once they take on a negotiating project—or any project, for that matter—CEOs make sure everything on the "hot list" gets taken care of. They can't afford to leave any loose ends in a negotiating session, and they commit to following through on all their commitments. You'll want to do the same. (Side note: *Every* CEO I interviewed for this book had some personalized strategy for making sure that nothing "fell through the cracks.")

Joe Gustafson, CEO of Brainshark, knows both sides of the "get it done" equation: "I'll run fast and far from salespeople and prospects who cannot clearly commit to what needs to be done." Moral: Before entering a negotiation, make your list and check it twice.

WISE NEGOTIATING TRAIT 3: KNOW WHEN TO ASK, NOT JUST WHAT TO ASK FOR

Successful CEOs know you can't reap what you don't sow. Their actions always seem to be in accordance with the "ebb and flow." They get involved early in important deals, they know when to wait, and they know when to push. This trait comes in handy in negotiating sessions.

> Follow through when you make a commitment to a CEO or a member of the CEO's team—no matter what. When you don't do as promised when promised, you give the competition the upper hand.

Emil Wang, CEO of Latitude Communications, attributes this trait to an ability to be involved throughout the sales process; he points out that the sales and negotiating functions are really interwoven. "You've always got to be 'closing' for something," he says. "I need to get involved early in the sales cycle. I can't wait until we're losing the deal or until we're at an impasse. I'm not big on waiting until the bottom of the ninth to get things done."

WISE NEGOTIATING TRAIT 4:
DON'T TAKE SHORTCUTS

> CEO success principle: Failure is the very best teacher. (Think about it: We rarely ask ourselves why we won.)

CEOs have certain values they just won't compromise. That's not to say they are stubborn, but they do know how, when, and where to draw a boundary. Ill-advised departures from guiding principles can carry huge costs, the most important of which are non-monetary: lower self-esteem, damaged reputation, and damaged self-reliance, to name just a few.

Keith McCumber, CEO of Daylight Systems Inc., has a core value that says, as he puts it, "Learn to recognize early on when we're looking at a situation in which we're unlikely to be successful. I allow people to fail,... but making the same mistake twice is out of the question." This translates, in his case, to highly focused negotiations and hardly any that drag on interminably.

WISE NEGOTIATING TRAIT 5:
TURN ENVY INTO ENERGY

Successful CEOs are happy with what they have and who they are. That doesn't mean they don't want to grow and prosper. They just know the importance of being happy with what is taking place in the here and now.

That may not seem like a trait for successful negotiation, but it is. Envy saps energy and poisons relationships; admiration of another's positive traits and accomplishments is a supreme compliment that helps you focus on what you need to improve in your life, business, relationships, finances—and negotiating posture.

Samuel Katz, CEO of Samuel Katz Inc., says: "Don't try to be a wise guy! Skip the typical sales *spiel*—which usually covers up something negative—and stay on purpose." Katz also points out that we tend to play power games with people we envy, and he advises against this. "Whenever you're in a negotiation, never, ever interrupt the person doing the talking." His reasoning? Interrupting looks like an attempt to shift the power, control, and authority away from the other person and onto you. This is not a good idea.

WISE NEGOTIATING TRAIT 6: AVOID THE OTHER PERSON'S PROBLEM(S)

This is a great (and simple) "negotiating tactic" that more than one of the CEOs I interviewed mentioned. It is also one I've used for nearly three decades of negotiating with CEOs and other high-level contacts.

> CEO selling principle: Don't take on your prospect's problems.

This tactic is all about not inheriting someone's unresolved problem as your own. If I had one dollar for every time I've heard, "We don't have that amount of money in our budget" or "We don't have a budget" or "Your price is too high" or "I don't have the authority" or "We can't move forward right now" or "We need this by no later than next Monday," I'd be a millionaire. Look at all of these typical responses once again, and you'll see that each is an attempt to put the buyer's issues onto the seller's list of problems.

Instead of fighting the problem, putting it off until "later on" in the negotiations, or throwing a new one into the mix, what would happen if you approached the problem from the standpoint of finding a solution? What if you acted as a consultant with the responsibility of finding an outcome that makes both sides happy?

Keith McCumber urges you to address all the issues whenever they come up. Prompt the issues, and don't pick up any baggage that doesn't belong to you. "Beware of any term or condition that is put off for later discussion. When someone says, 'We can discuss this at a later point—I don't see this condition as being a big problem,' watch out!" This "insignificant" issue is very likely the deal breaker that will be rolled across the table when time is running out for you the seller (i.e., it's getting close to the end of your quarter or fiscal year, or some other important deadline is looming). CEOs and other effective negotiators know that people tend to become much more flexible when time is running out.

Heed McCumber's warning. Don't wait until "later." Deal with the issues now.

WISE NEGOTIATING TRAIT 7: THE CEO SWAGGER

To think, sell, and negotiate like a CEO, you must understand that, more than anyone else in a given organization, the CEO has the ultimate walk-away power.

> CEO selling principle: There are times when walking away from a sale is the right thing to do.

The power to walk away is the most profound negotiating tactic a CEO will use. They basically say, "I am totally willing to pass on this opportunity." There is a big difference between that way of thinking and the way of thinking that says, "I am going to get the price as low as I can before I buy." Walk-away power takes the opportunity past the point of "no return." The winning party will convince the other party that his/her side *can and will* walk away from the negotiations. Keep in mind that the goal here is *not* to actually "walk" but to get the other side to do what you want.

Joe Mancuso points out that there are two effective ways to protect yourself against this tactic.

1. *Increase your options.* If you're looking to contract with a business consultant, for instance, make sure you've got at

least one other business consultant that you would hire. This way, when it comes to "walking" on the first one, you've got a backup.

2. *Don't give up too much too early in the buying process.* The point here is that "give and take" makes much more sense than "give and give and give and give some more." If you and the buyer/seller both invest roughly equivalent amounts of time and energy in the relationship, you're less likely to run into the "walkaway" tactic in the bottom of the ninth inning.

> CEO success principle: Keep your business relationships balanced. Make sure your business partners and prospects are taking steps when you do.

WISE NEGOTIATING TRAIT 8: ASK FOR THE STARS

Asking for more than the other side expects (moving beyond expectations) is a great negotiating trait of the successful CEO. If you're a salesperson, you may already be conditioned within the "do whatever it takes to get the sale" mentality. CEOs know this. Don't let them take undue advantage of that mind-set. Ask for something extravagant yourself. By doing so, you'll be modeling an important successful CEO negotiating trait.

Consider This

- Asking for more than is expected is one of the only ways to establish perceived value beyond actual value. For example, ask your prospect CEO if he or she would be willing to be used as a reference within three months or as soon as the buying organization receives its expected result, whichever comes first.

- Asking for more than is expected gives a CEO room to "wiggle." She/he can always lower expectations later on. In the spirit of marketing mobility (see Chapter 15), ask your prospect CEO to allow your products to be included in their quarterly newsletter to their customer base.

- Asking for more than is expected tends to prevent "dead-locks" in negotiations because it promotes free discussion of the most important issues early on in the process. For instance, asking for payment upon receipt of order rather than waiting the normal 30 days will help with your organization's net working capital and put a little healthy pressure on the buying organization. It also gives you something interesting to talk about early on.

- Asking for more than is expected will almost always create a feeling that the other person has won when the expectations are lowered. Accepting net 30 in the above case will almost always make the "buying" CEO happy—which is the way he or she ought to be.

Secrets of VITO

THINK

Believe it or not, CEOs start negotiating during the first meeting they have with any new prospect. They know that too much is lost if you wait until the last minute. During the very first meeting you have with a target CEO, make sure you present your standard terms and conditions; be sure to highlight any of the terms that are "cast in concrete." Setting the expectations of what's possible and what's not is a great way to keep a good deal from going south, and it's also a great strategy for making sure you don't spend too much time on the wrong deals.

SELL

Here are some CEO negotiating traits that you should adopt at the *beginning* of every new business relationship.

> *Pick your battles carefully.* Even the most valiant fight may not be worth the potential loss it entails. Make sure you assign a value or

a realistic dollar amount to each and every new opportunity before you spend too much time on it.

➤ *Eliminate loose ends.* Once you take on a negotiating project—or any project, for that matter—make sure everything on the list gets taken care of. If you neglect a (seemingly) minor issue, you may pay for that neglect at the end of the negotiating process.

➤ *Know when to ask, not just what to ask for.* You must know when to wait and when to push. Consider the following dialogue:

> Target CEO: *Your price is too high.*
>
> You: *Yes, it does seem high, doesn't it?*

Don't say another word. Your target CEO will tell you all you need to know to move forward.

➤ *Don't take shortcuts.* Ill-advised departures from guiding principles can carry huge costs for yourself and your organization. Know where you've got "wiggle room"—and where you don't.

➤ *Turn envy into energy.* As soon as envy takes hold, people get protective, jealous, and rigid. You can't afford these traits during negotiation discussions.

➤ *Never assume the other person's problem(s).* Consider this simple illustration:

> Target CEO: *We can't move forward right now.*
>
> You: *That's unfortunate. Your organization will be missing out on....*

Any other "typical" response ("What can we do to make the offer more attractive?") will get you nowhere. Don't start negotiating against yourself. Never adopt the other side's problems.

➤ *Swagger when you can.* The power to walk away is the most profound negotiating tactic of all. Effective CEOs are masters at using this strategy; basically they say, "I am quite willing to pass on this opportunity." The question then becomes—*will* they?

➤ *Ask for the stars.* Be careful not to rely too much on the "do whatever it takes to get the sale" mentality. CEOs know how to take undue advantage of that mind-set. Ask for something extravagant yourself. By doing so, you'll be modeling an important CEO negotiating trait.

TAKE ACTION

Make a list of all the negotiating outcomes in the past year that had a result that was less than desirable for you. When your list is complete, highlight the issues that could have been solved by using one or more of the tactics listed previously.

21

"Drive thy business or it will drive thee."

BENJAMIN FRANKLIN

BE THE CEO!

A t the beginning of this book, we established that a majority of the CEOs and top officers running businesses in America were once salespeople. They prospected for new business, probed for needs, made presentations, sent out proposals, handled objections, and, yes, went for the "close."

We also identified several operating principles, personality traits, and styles that salespeople share with the CEOs and top officers of an enterprise. Let's take one last look at these guiding principles—and get some advice from the top on how to become more self-assured in thinking and selling like a CEO.

As you read what follows, keep in mind that self-assurance is one of the cornerstones of a CEO's life. CEOs are *self-directed to overachievement.* It's the critical ingredient that will lead you to

---

success in sales—or anywhere else in the business world you desire to go, up to and including the CEO's corner office.

1: CEOs WHO SELL KNOW THEIR IDEAL PROSPECTS

> Be self-directed. Know where you're going, how long it's going to take you to get there, and what you intend to do upon your arrival.

CEOs hate wasting time, so they target the people and groups *most likely to buy from them.* Wasted time in the sales process adds to the cost of sales and extends the critical time-to-revenue benchmark. Wasted time also gets shareholders and board members breathing down the CEO's neck. The higher the cost of sales and the longer the time to revenue, the lower the profit margin.

Bob Palmisano, CEO of MacroChem, learned about targeting ideal prospects early on at Bausch & Lomb, Playtex, and Mobil Oil. "You must figure out very quickly how you fit in with a given prospect," he advises. "Back away quickly when what you have doesn't fit what they need."

This is not typically what salespeople do. "Beating the dead horse" and forecasting low-probability deals are all too common among salespeople who *don't* sell like CEOs. Palmisano feels very strongly that his salespeople must not have the attitude of "doing anything to make the numbers." Given this fact, it's not surprising that Palmisano's definition of failure is "doing deals that don't work out."

Take Palmisano's advice to the bank: Keep your sales cycle short and to the point. "Stay 'on message' in a sales call," he suggests, "and stick to a shortlist of two or three value propositions that you know you can deliver." If you've got a match, pull all the stops out and go for it.

The Bottom Line

Don't waste your time talking to prospects that have nothing, or very little, in common with your best customers. If you haven't yet completed your template of ideal prospects, you're not thinking and selling like a CEO.

Reality Check

Salesperson: *"So—how does this sound to you?"*

Prospect CEO: *"I don't quite see how it fits at this time."*

Salesperson: *"Shall I contact you next month?"*

Prospect CEO: *"Why not make it at the end of next quarter."*

Salesperson: *"Great. I'll contact you then."*

The salesperson then sets the phone down, pulls up the forecast report, and types: "ABC Inc. Value: $250K. Probability: 50 percent. Next, it's out the door for a long lunch."

Don't fool yourself, your manager, or your own CEO. Begin thinking and selling like a CEO by being brutally honest about what's really going on in any given business relationship. Empty your forecast of all of your deadbeat prospects—and make room for the real ones.

> Be ready to ask: "If I were one of your top salespeople, how would you want me to proceed?"

2: CEOs USE SIMILAR CRITERIA TO BUY AND SELL

CEOs take the same energetic, visionary approach to buying that they do to selling. Once you see a CEO make a buying decision, you'll know a lot about how that person approaches selling (and vice versa).

If you were to pick up the telephone and call Mike Borer, CEO of Xcel Pharmaceuticals, you would most likely get shunted to one of Borer's direct reports. Why? Because Borer's strong background in finance tells him that "ownership and accountability while following the chain of command" is what works. He believes in his people and trusts them to help him in both the buying and the selling process. He has to. The organization he leads operates in a market where strict government regulation is the norm. Therefore, he looks for tight specifications and high degrees of accuracy in all value propositions that come his way, and he gets lots of help from the team.

Work *with* the CEO's buying and selling criteria—don't fight them.

What turns Borer off faster than a speeding bullet is when a salesperson who calls on him "lacks a sense of entitlement." Borer's advice on selling and success is based on his own expectations of his team, his organization, and his products. "Pride, ownership, accountability, and drive" are what he looks for. Translation: You best be at your best when you call Borer.

The Bottom Line

Don't forget: How a given CEO buys will mirror how the same CEO sells to his or her marketplace.

Before you make any attempt to pick a CEO prospect to sell to, find out a little about what it is that they sell. If they sell the cheapest "widgets" in town, and you've got the most expensive solution to offer, think twice before you devote yourself to "researching" this account any further. You may waste a lot of time and energy.

Reality Check
Meaningful research (What does this company sell and how?) is more helpful than *endless* research (What is the history of the company over the past 150 years?). Focus on the former.

3: CEOs AVOID BUCK-PASSING AND LIKE HAVING THE FINAL SAY

Even when they delegate, successful CEOs are the final approvers of every initiative with which they come in contact. "Directors" (their direct reports) are empowered to conduct the fact-finding and make decisions/recommendations, which the CEO must approve. They manage a tight circle of influence and authority.

Here's what Andrew Horowitz, CEO of The Estate Management Group, has to say on this topic. "My persistence and my ability to identify and clarify set the pace in my organization. Everything echoes back to me."

Horowitz never settles for what he calls a "stopper" in a sales situation or decision process. As he puts it, "Failure is quitting." His organization deals with high-net-worth individuals, and he sees his job clearly: "My only job is to make my customers rich—not keep them from becoming poor." Horowitz takes final responsibility in a dramatic way, no matter how much he delegates. You should, too.

The Bottom Line

If what you have to offer the marketplace can touch one or more of the following areas in the CEO's world, you can bet your sale on the fact that the CEO will have the final say. Those areas are:

- revenue.
- efficiencies and effectiveness.
- protection of existing customers and market share.
- add-on business from that existing base.
- cutting nonvalue expense.

> Help CEOs overachieve any current strategic initiative—and you'll win both their loyalty and their business.

Reality Check

Remember—if you don't start your sales cycle at the top, you're not thinking and selling like a CEO. Sure, it might be easier at first to get the attention of an office manager, but after that initial call, the process will slow down, costing you time, money, and the sale. You've got to get to the CEO and find out what your chances are of doing business before you spend any of your precious time with anyone else. Ask the top person where you stand, and you'll get a straight answer.

4: CEOs WHO SELL MODEL THE IDEAL SALES PROCESS PERSONALLY AND CONSISTENTLY

Who plays the role of a model salesperson better than the head of the company? No one. (*Every* CEO I interviewed agreed with me on this point.)

The Bottom Line

Here are some important thoughts on modeling the ideal sales process from the CEOs I interviewed for this book.

> *Yes, you need to sell, but you don't need to sell to everyone."*
>
> —Samuel Katz, CEO of Samuel Katz Inc.
>
> (He was emphasizing the importance of focusing on the right prospect.)

> *Follow-up and persistence is critical. Answer and return all phone calls.*
>
> —Doug Simon, CEO, Mobility Elevator & Lift Co.

> *Forget the typical 'ice-breaker.' Get down to the real business issues first.*
>
> —Keith McCumber, CEO, Daylight Systems

> *Storytelling is an extremely effective way to make your point. It also adds creditability and social proof to your claims.*
>
> —Joe Sugarman, CEO, JS&A Group

> *Never perform any activity in the sales process that doesn't give a payback.*
>
> —Fred W. Green, CEO

> *Blitz your territory.*
>
> —Cash Nickerson, CEO, Team America

(Note: A territory blitz is a concentrated effort to reach out and contact a high number of prospects or existing customers. You can do it by sending a letter or e-mail first and then picking up the telephone or making a series of in-person calls. How many territory blitzes have you performed in the past three months? If your answer is none, go back and reread chapters 4 through 10 of this book.)

Always ask permission before you start to take notes. It lets the other person know that what they're saying is important to remember, and it clears issues of confidentiality.

—Joe Mancuso, CEO, The CEO Club

(Note: Mancuso's advice is dead-on; asking permission in this way actually builds EBS. How you ask permission has more to do with the tone of your voice and your body language than with the grammatical structure of the sentence you use—in other words, you can "ask permission" by making a tactful statement. My personal favorite strategy, which I used during my interviews for this book, sounds like this: "I'll be taking notes during our conversation; if you want me to strike anything out, let me know.")

Never improvise, never exaggerate. If you don't know something, quickly admit it.

—Law Larson, CEO, Secure Media Products

Aim high. It's best to cast a bigger net into your territory.

—Kevin Dyevich, CEO, Comfort Direct

(Note: Think of the last big deal you landed, take the total time you worked on it, and divide that by the amount of the sale or the amount of your commission check. Now do the same with the smallest sale you made. Compare the numbers. If you're honest, you'll find that big deals are more worthy of your time and effort.)

> Selling means communicating effectively with your prospects and customers.

Always be clear on the fact that you are here to sell.

—Bob Posten, CEO, Landis Strategy & Innovation

Reality Check

If you're not selling, you're not serving your organization. If you're not thinking and selling like a successful CEO, you're not serving your prospect. How much of your time each day or week is spent "face to face" with your prospects and customers? Take the time to create a log and record for the next 30 days what you're spending your time on. What's the ratio? Are you spending most of your time involved in prospect and customer contact? If not, what changes can be made?

5: CEOs WHO SELL ESTABLISH PERSONAL VISIBILITY WITHIN THE MARKETPLACE AND THE COMMUNITY AS A WHOLE

Pay your dues. Join the groups and organizations that will win you the exposure you need.

You'll recall Jennifer Ash, CEO of Tomco Tool & Die, a female CEO in an industry dominated by men. Jennifer had to learn about metallurgy, the marketplace, her company, and how to relate to her prospects and customers. And she had to do it all quickly. She pulled it off. Ash's advice on how to do what she did is direct and to the point: "Join a professional organization that relates to what it is you're selling."

Become visible in your community of potential prospects and existing customers. Volunteer your time to a professional organization and get on the mailing list of associations whose members can purchase your products.

The Bottom Line

Tonight, surf the 'Net and find five associations and professional organizations that relate to what you sell. Join all five.

Reality Check

Consider this: If you don't join organizations like these, someone at one of your competitors will.

6: CEOs WHO SELL PERSONALLY MONITOR CHANGES IN THEIR MARKETPLACE

Sure, this is extra work for the ordinary salesperson. But CEOs don't make themselves available to ordinary salespeople.

One of the fastest ways to increase your value to your prospects and customers is to know what's changing in your marketplace. CEOs pay big bucks for consultants to provide "trend analysis." You should provide it for free.

Joe Mancuso, CEO of the CEO Club, gives us the most hard-hitting advice in this area. I'll quote one of his best-selling books (he's written a total of 24), *How to Write a Winning Business Plan* (Simon and Schuster).

"Become a super information processor; open all of your mail, watch the telephone log, read the business journal, spot a growth industry, organize a customer focus group, travel, and attend."

> CEO selling principle: Nothing can replace the right activity; nothing wastes more time than the wrong activity.

The Bottom Line

Here is what Mancuso is telling you and me to do.

- *Go* to the lobby of your company. Look at the visitor's log and ask yourself, Who is a supplier to my organization that could become one of my prospects? Do this with every organization you have as a customer, too.
- *Keep* your eyes peeled for upstarts and emerging industries. It's a feather in your cap to pass along some interesting information to the next prospect CEO you call on.
- *Call* five of your best customers and ask them to lunch all together at the same time. You may want to ask your CEO or vice president of product development to join you. Before the lunch is over, pick a date one month out and invite everyone back.
- *Take* a different way back to your office and take note of what you see. How many new business parks and buildings

are being constructed? Stop in the leasing office and ask for the names of the companies that are moving in. Don't wait—call them immediately and introduce yourself.

- *Show* up and attend chamber of commerce meetings in your territory. It's a great way to meet CEOs and other business owners.

> The law of "reciprocity" will always kick in when it comes to building the relationship with your target CEO. Listen while they are talking, and they will listen to you. Give them value beyond what they paid for, and they'll figure out how to return the favor in referrals and add-on business.

Reality Check
Again—if you don't do this, don't be surprised if the competition does.

7: CEOs WHO SELL CONSTANTLY BUILD ON INTERPERSONAL RELATIONSHIPS TO SECURE ONE-ON-ONE LOYALTY FROM CUSTOMERS

Bob Posten, CEO of Landis Strategy & Innovation, put it this way: "I had to get real about what I was doing for my customers. I had to use what I was selling. Then was I able to articulate what I did accurately to my prospects and customers."

Once Posten did that, he earned the loyalty of his customers and was able to build new market share quickly for his business. Posten is an expert at building loyalty by making *deposits* into the "relationship bank account," not withdrawals.

The Bottom Line
Be loyal to your customers on a personal level, and they'll return the favor.

Reality Check
How many customers have you lost in the past year? Ask yourself, Why did they leave? What could I have

done to prevent it? What would happen if I called them right now and asked them to come back?

8: CEOs WHO SELL LOOK FOR A
BALANCED "GAIN" EQUATION

Basically, this means delivering and receiving enhanced value. Each and every CEO I interviewed was quite keen on the topic of value.

As Peter Shea, the owner and CEO of Entrepreneur Media (the publishers of this book, *Entrepreneur* magazine, Entrepreneur.com and Entrepreneur Radio), put it, "I find that a fellow CEO will quickly understand the value we can offer— once I make an effort to speak his or her language. And I do. I check my ego; I put the other person first." In other words, *getting* enhanced value means *giving* enhanced value, on terms the other person can quickly appreciate.

The Bottom Line

Learning how to put your value in front of your prospect and customer CEOs is critical to your success.

Reality Check

Don't let anyone kid you. Conveying your value takes practice. Find five prospects that are smaller than one of your major target companies but that are in the correct target industry. Run your CEO-contact campaign in exactly the same way you are planning to run it for your "real" target company. Go ahead and make your mistakes on the smaller, less important potential prospects. Ask each of the five CEO prospects you approach what they thought

> The upside of your business proposition must outweigh the downside, or your target CEO will not do business with you.

of the content of your letter, telephone opening statement, and/or voice-mail message. When you're satisfied with your test results, up-shift to larger and more important companies until you're ready to reach out to your target company CEO.

9: CEOs WHO SELL MAKE INTELLIGENT DECISIONS QUICKLY AND INDEPENDENTLY

People who are capable of making quick decisions usually have extremely high levels of self-reliance.

Joel Ronning, CEO of Digital River, makes decisions for his company based on a fascinating equation: "Experience + Intelligence = Intuition." To this, Ronning adds a high degree of fearlessness and puts the all-important element of *time* in front of every decision he makes. In other words, *when* does a given outcome have to take place? *What* has to happen before then? *What* choices must be made now in order to bring about the necessary results?

The Bottom Line

Follow Ronning's lead. Focus on *when* your outcome needs to take place, *what* has to happen beforehand, and *what* processes are under your control right now to make the results you want happen.

Reality Check

> Focus is to everyday thinking as a laser is to the beam of a flashlight.

If you have trouble making decisions quickly and independently, you may need to work on increasing your own level of self-reliance. (Negative mental self-talk, like "I can't," "I should have," "I could have," or "It's not my job," are common symptoms of low self-reliance.) You can build self-reliance by focusing consciously and vividly on your past successes and by taking personal, solitary time to come up with answers to tough questions.

10: CEOs WHO SELL STAY FOCUSED AND LIKE PEOPLE WHO CAN DO THE SAME

Isn't it amazing what the power of focus can accomplish? In the field of medicine, a focused beam of light performs laser surgery that is less intrusive and less destructive than doctors could have dreamed possible 30 years ago. In manufacturing, specialized systems that focus on efficiency have helped save several American industries from succumbing to offshore competition. In sales—and your own career—you have the opportunity to take the power of focus and use it to change everything.

Emil Wang, CEO of Latitude Communications, is big on focus. "Come at me with what you're selling, be honest, and stay on purpose," he says. "Be very clear as to what you want from me, and don't ask me premature questions. If any salesperson, or anyone else for that matter, sounds 'flaky,' I'll dust them off." If that doesn't motivate you to further your own agenda by sticking to the target CEOs, I don't know what will.

The Bottom Line

Stay on point—don't get distracted.

Reality Check

By my estimation, successful CEOs spend about 75 percent of their "developmental energy" in a specific field of expertise. Twenty percent is spent on development of new talents that relate to their core strengths. Like all of us, they must spend some small amount of time—and perhaps 5 percent of their attention— engaged in areas that are outside their core competency.

Take my advice and follow the lead of CEOs who sell. When it comes to relating to them, stay away from that last 5 percent. Deal only with the areas *they* care about, the skills and capacities *they* want to expand. Learn how to be an agent of change within *their* area of expertise—as an expert who complements their world view—and you'll earn a spot in their day.

Secrets of VITO

THINK

> ➤ *Take an inventory.* Identify which of the ten operating principles discussed in this chapter are already close to second nature for you.

Review the following affirmations closely; then write them down and post them where you'll see them every day.

> ➤ "I will back away quickly when I know that what I have doesn't fit what the other person needs."
> ➤ "I will have pride in what I sell, take ownership of each sale, and be accountable for the end result."
> ➤ "Everything I do echoes back to me."
> ➤ "Yes, I need to sell, but I don't need to sell to everyone."
> ➤ "I will join and participate in professional organizations that relate to what I sell."
> ➤ "I am a superior information processor."
> ➤ "I actually use what I sell whenever possible."
> ➤ "I check my ego at the door and put the other person first."
> ➤ "I will use my intuition to help me sell."

SELL

Here's another easy-to-implement idea that will help you sell like a CEO: Stay on target with prospects!

Without hijacking the conversation, be clear as to exactly what you want from the next prospect you approach. Set appropriate goals for the outcomes of the meeting or discussion. At an appropriate point in the

---

meeting, outline those goals and outcomes without apology or hesitation and solicit the CEO's input.

TAKE ACTION

Designate one business day each week to one of the affirmations you've written down. Continue this process for at least 30 days or until you see results that follow your affirmations.

22

---

*"Opportunity is seeing what everybody else sees,
and thinking what nobody else has thought."*

—Peter Shea

The Freedom of Entrepreneurship

S ome people define *entrepreneur* as "one who organizes, operates, and, especially, assumes the risk of a business venture."

Every CEO I interviewed for this book fits that
description. And so do the best salespeople. We
are organizers, operators, and risk-takers. Each
sales territory can be seen as a "business venture."
It has every operating component that a business
has: human and capital assets, fixed and variable
expenses, and revenue potential. Its product is
"revenue," and its marketplace is what is being
sold within a geographic area or named account
list. It has a CEO (the salesperson) who is in
charge of the mission statement and all other
strategic and tactical operational considerations.

> Fear has no
> place in sales. If
> you fear losing,
> you'll not be
> able to take
> the necessary
> risks to make
> the sale.

THE BRASS RING

Start by getting some insights from the CEO of the organization that probably knows more about entrepreneurship than any other in America. Entrepreneur Media gets and holds the attention of 3.7 million risk-takers every month; it's run by a CEO who is probably the "entrepreneur of entrepreneurs," Peter Shea.

"It takes a certain amount of courage," Shea points out, "to become an entrepreneur. First of all, you have to be willing to get on the carousel, find a horse that's on the edge, and reach way out for the 'brass ring.' Once you have that ring, you must be willing to take tons of risk and use it."

Shea's journey to success has been a long one that's featured its fair share of risk. "Basically," he says, "I'm unemployable." (This is a trait that many maverick entrepreneurs share.) "I was fired from two jobs which I was quite successful at." After that came two unsuccessful attempts at start-ups.

"You can't be afraid to lose," Shea advises. "And the fact that you do lose now and then doesn't make you a loser." The real measurement of success for Shea—and every other extremely successful businessperson I've met—involves stamina and a willingness to look to the long term. As he puts it, "My wins are a lot bigger than my losses."

> The kind of courage it takes to be an entrepreneur is closely allied to the kind of courage it takes to be a great salesperson.

OTHERWISE UNEMPLOYABLE—AND PROUD OF IT

Many successful salespeople are (let's face it) unemployable, or at least hard to employ, in other areas of the company. They're a different breed, in part because they tend to be ego-driven. That's not a slam on salespeople; it's a fact of life, and an important parallel between salespeople and senior executives.

Ego pushes you to achievement. Ego distinguishes you from "the rest of the pack." Ego makes it possible to turn thinking into action and pushes you to reach way out past the edge and grab for that "brass ring." Ego is what helps you move past fear.

GROW OR DIE

This may sound harsh, but being a successful entrepreneur means you'll never really "retire" from the game. And the same, I think, is true for successful salespeople. Truly successful people never stop growing and learning. When they get to the top of their mountain, they have a way of helping others to get to the top of theirs as they push even harder for the next summit.

THE YOUTH MOVEMENT

According to Entrepreneur Media's research, the entrepreneur of today is younger than just ten years ago. Why? Here's the theory.

> Presenting the right question to your brain is just as important as presenting the right question to your target CEO.

In the past, executives who found themselves "outplaced" by mergers, acquisitions, and re-engineering had both money and time, so they started their own businesses. Nowadays, there are a lot more choices for everyone. Franchises, network marketing opportunities, internet ventures, and lower-end investment technologies have combined to help make entrepreneurship a pathway of choice, not necessity.

A similar dynamic applies to salespeople. Today's rank and file is younger, and often more formally educated, than the salesperson of a few decades ago. Many universities now have degree programs in sales (for example, The Fisher Institute for Professional Selling at Ohio's University of Akron). More and more people are *choosing* selling as a career, and societal perceptions about selling are changing. The selling profession is finally shaking itself free from the snake-oil stereotypes of yesteryear. And that's a great trend. It points toward exactly what *I've* been pointing you toward in this book: taking what you do for a living to a level of professionalism that's equal to that of any entrepreneur—any CEO.

PUTTING ALL YOUR RESOURCES INTO PLAY

Ready for a shocking statistic? According to Entrepreneur Media's research, a mere 1 percent of the nation's entrepreneurial population has actually realized its business dreams and revenue-generating potential to the fullest.

How about you? What do you plan to do with the information and strategies you've gleaned from this book?

Give yourself a chance to review the material again. I'd recommend skimming the book for a "recharge" on key points and concepts at least every 60 days. When you next review this material, keep an eye on the actual *quotes* from CEOs. Have you noticed any common themes?

I showed this manuscript to a dear friend of mine, Kathleen Brooks. She holds a PhD in psychology, has a successful practice in San Diego, and is authoring a fascinating new book, *Choosing Maturity: 21 Ways to Become a Real Adult.* Here's what Kathleen had to say about the quotes from CEOs that she read in this book:

> *There is no doubt that these individuals would score extremely high in being self-assured and having a high degree of self-esteem.*

There's a commonality between successful CEOs and successful salespeople.

Here are some other success traits I noticed about the CEOs I interviewed for this book. All, I know, are worth modeling.

Asking Themselves Positively Framed Questions

The CEOs I interviewed asked questions like, "What makes me and my organization unique and special?" They avoided asking themselves questions like, "Why is there so much !@#$% competition in this marketplace?"

> Entrepreneurs turn thinking and dreaming into action and living.

The human brain will research any and all questions put before it. If we put our brains to work searching for an answer to a presupposition that is not conducive to prosperous growth, our brains will provide lots of answers that will pound self-assurance and self-esteem into the ground.

Build your self-assurance and self-esteem by posing CEO-like, positively framed questions to yourself. Focus on uplifting, positive, reinforcing, creative questions. ("How did I get such a great opportunity?" "What can I do to change this situation for the better?")

If you do this, you'll get answers, intuitions, and breakthroughs that you never thought yourself capable of.

Setting the Right Expectations

The CEOs I interviewed exceeded their own expectations remarkably often. This isn't because they're smarter or work harder than anyone else. It's simply because their enthusiasm is set higher than their expectations.

Their core enthusiasm comes from being excited about whatever it is they happen to be doing. It's no secret that when you set enthusiasm at the highest possible level, you automatically establish (or re-establish) positive expectations for yourself.

The moral: Focus on whatever reward, emotional state, place, person, or accomplishment *gets you pumped up.* Do it habitually, and do it *consciously*—until you're doing it without even having to think about it, just as a CEO would do.

Adopting the Right Attitude for the Situation

CEOs know that mindless good cheer only goes so far. It's more important to have the best possible, realistic attitude for any given situation.

The people I interviewed all understood that attitudes must be consciously cultivated and must change as conditions warrant.

Begin today to carefully observe your situation and consciously select an attitude that fits. Do this by using all your senses to evaluate all the circumstances of what's actually going on around you. When you begin taking conscious control of your attitude and "programming" yourself with attitudes like "conscious," "alert," "detail-oriented," and "celebratory," you'll have more mental and intellectual energy at your disposal to think clearly about the tasks at hand.

Gathering the Right Evidence

Successful CEOs constantly gather evidence to support key assumptions about themselves and whatever business or personal challenges happen to be on their plate at the time.

> Focus on that which quickly and dramatically changes your emotional state for the better.

The key word here is "support"—because whenever we're not thinking and selling like a CEO, we're apt to focus on the evidence that confirms the worst about ourselves. ("I lost that sale—what a dummy I am!" "I didn't get the promotion to senior sales executive—there must be something wrong with me.")

The CEOs I interviewed developed the ability to consistently present evidence that was supportive and nurturing in content.

When things go right, *focus clearly on what happened and use that as evidence* to reinforce your most positive traits. When results aren't what you had hoped for or expected, ask yourself, "Which one of my own positive traits *didn't* I use that could have changed the outcome?" Find an answer, then make a point of bringing that trait into the forefront of your daily activities so you'll get a better outcome next time.

CONGRATULATIONS!

On page eight of this book I promised you that when you reached this point you would know how to calculate risk, focus on rewards, and get the results you deserve from your sales efforts. Well, what do you think? Have you been given ample information on how to think and sell like a CEO? Have you completed the exercises I suggested? Have you checked out www.CEOsellingtips.com? If not, it's still here waiting for you. If you have taken all of these important steps, then I congratulate you! My only request is that you share your newfound knowledge with someone you care about so they in turn can realize for themselves that selling to the top really is fun!

Secrets of VITO

THINK

There is no doubt that these individuals would score extremely high in being self-assured and having a high degree of self-esteem.

That's what Kathleen Brooks (who holds a PhD in psychology) said about the traits of successful CEOs who sell.

SELL

Notice once again what you have in common with successful CEOs— and how these traits have supported you thus far in your own career:

- ➤ Entrepreneurial spirit
- ➤ Willingness to take risks
- ➤ Courage
- ➤ Eagerness to grow and learn

TAKE ACTION

Give yourself a chance to review the material again. I'd recommend skimming the book for a "recharge" on key points and concepts at least every 60 days. Think about creating a company called "Me Incorporated." It won't be traded on the stock market, but it will increase in value every day. Why? Because, if you do what it takes to make "Me Incorporated" an industry leader, you will:

➤ consciously use and reinforce your best emotional and intellectual characteristics.

➤ have unyielding enthusiasm.

➤ live your day with an appropriate, deliberately chosen attitude that fits the circumstance.

➤ continually find and highlight the supporting evidence you need to promote health, wealth, and happiness.

By doing this consistently, you'll outshine all your competition, and you'll emerge as the leader you were always meant to be.

AFTERWORD

I wrote this book for one purpose: to give you freedom. Now that you've got it, use it!

Salespeople sell products and services every day to organizations that have the freedom to choose whom they buy from.

Now that you've finished this book, you, too, have a choice. You don't have to start at the bottom. You don't have to sell like you belong at the bottom. You can sell at the *top*.

Now that you know how to do that, don't give up your freedom. Don't give up your right to call, build business relationships with, and add value to *anyone* in any organization.

Now that you know how to think and sell like a CEO, there's no excuse to act any other way.

—*Anthony Parinello*

A DIRECT OFFER FROM ME TO YOU

Your investment in this book entitles you to privileged, VIP access to my one-of-a-kind e-learning center. This unique center provides:

- *Nonstop learning opportunities.* Learn and prosper at your own pace in the convenience of your home or office, via the World Wide Web.

  - Regularly up-dated e-lessons that expand upon the information in this book.

  - Downloadable worksheets.

  - 7 x 24 x 365 unlimited access.

- A monthly e-newsletter titled: VITO Wire that provides on-going insights to how CEO's think and sell.

- Access to live, internet broadcasts.

- Additional discounts on other C-level selling books, audio and e-learning programs

Visit www.CEOsellingtips.com for complete details.

MEET THE AUTHOR

Anthony Parinello is one of the nation's top sales trainers and motivational speakers. To inquire about his speaking schedule and availability, visit his web site or call his office.

www.vitoselling.com

or call

(800) 777-8486

YOUR OPINION COUNTS

To give your opinion on the contents of this book, e-mail the author at www.vitoselling.com and click on: Contact Us then click on: e-mail Tony.

I WANT TO HEAR FROM YOU!

I want to hear about what think of this book! If you have any comments or suggestions on how my work can be improved, please take the time to write them out and send them to me at:

Anthony Parinello
c/o Entrepreneur Media
2445 McCabe Way, Suite 400
Irvine, California 92614

INDEX